THE WILES LECTURES GIVEN AT
THE QUEEN'S UNIVERSITY BELFAST

# PHILOSOPHERS OF
# PEACE AND WAR

# PHILOSOPHERS OF PEACE AND WAR

## KANT, CLAUSEWITZ, MARX ENGELS AND TOLSTOY

### W. B. GALLIE

PROFESSOR OF POLITICAL SCIENCE
UNIVERSITY OF CAMBRIDGE

## CAMBRIDGE UNIVERSITY PRESS

CAMBRIDGE
LONDON · NEW YORK · MELBOURNE

Published by the Syndics of the Cambridge University Press
The Pitt Building, Trumpington Street, Cambridge CB2 1RP
Bentley House, 200 Euston Road, London NW1 2DB
32 East 57th Street, New York, NY 10022, USA

First published 1978
Reprinted 1979

First printed in Great Britain by
Western Printing Services Ltd, Bristol

Reprinted and bound in Great Britain by
Redwood Burn Limited
Trowbridge & Esher

*Library of Congress Cataloguing in Publication Data*
Gallie, W. B. 1912–
Philosophers of peace and war.

(The Wiles lectures)
Bibliography: p.
1. Peace – Addresses, essays, lectures. 2. War –
Addresses, essays, lectures. 3. Clausewitz, Karl von,
1780–1831 – Addresses, essays, lectures. 4. Engels,
Friedrich, 1820–1895 – Addresses, essays, lectures,
5. Kant, Immanuel, 1724–1804 – Addresses, essays,
lectures. 7. Tolstoi, Lev Nikolaevich, graf, 1828–1910
– Addresses, essays, lectures. I. Title. II. Series.

JX1963.G23   327′.172   77–23553
ISBN 0 521 21779 2

*To my daughter Didi*
*this book is gratefully dedicated*

Wo aber Gefahr ist, wächst
Das Rettende auch.
Hölderlin, *Patmos*

# CONTENTS

# PREFACE

This book contains, in slightly extended form, the Wiles Lectures which I delivered in the Queen's University, Belfast, in May 1976. My first and pleasant duty, therefore, is to express my gratitude to Mrs Janet Boyd and the other Trustees of the Wiles Foundation, for inviting me to the lectureship. They thus did me a signal honour, and also supplied me with a motive for presenting in generally assimilable form some results of my research and reflection over the last ten years.

An important feature of the Wiles Lectures is that a number of scholars, eminent in fields connected with the topic chosen, are invited to attend and to lead the discussion which follows each lecture. I was very fortunate in those who were invited to hear and to comment on my lectures. Mr B. J. Bond corrected my account of Clausewitz in a number of important places, and also alerted me to the flow of important books on Clausewitz which were to appear in the succeeding six weeks. (I refer to those of Professor Raymond Aron and Professor Peter Paret, and to the new translation of *On War* by Professor Paret and Mr Michael Howard.) Professor J. J. Lee had already called my attention to the extensive literature in German on the Marxists' reception of Clausewitz; for which I am greatly indebted to him. My gratitude to Professor A. J. M. Milne and Professor Ernest Gellner is of a deeper and more general kind. Both have unfailingly encouraged me in the researches which lie behind this book. Among many other lessons, Professor Milne first persuaded me of the importance of Kant's political philosophy, both for the history of political thought and for understanding Kant's philosophy as a whole; while Professor Gellner, through his writings and his loyal friendship, has sustained me in the belief that a philosopher is not necessarily precluded from the discussion of vital important questions. To these names, I must add those of two older scholars, from whom I have learnt much in recent years. In a number of places in the chapters that follow I express my indebtedness to

Professor F. H. Hinsley's expositions of Kant's theory of international relations, without which I could hardly have made headway in that obscure but (as I believe) immensely important field. Professor Sir Herbert Butterfield has given me, over the years, the greatest possible encouragement, always understanding what I was trying to do, and impressing upon me that I must never confuse what war has made of men with what historians have made of war.

Among many others who have helped me with this book in ways too various to be mentioned here, I would like to thank those who have so patiently typed and re-typed my manuscript, in particular Mrs Lesley Bower, Secretary of the Social and Political Sciences Committee at Cambridge, and Mrs Hazel Dunn, the Fellows' Secretary at Peterhouse.

Since, as I mention in Chapter 2, this book is primarily a commentary on a number of outstanding, yet difficult, incomplete and confusing texts, I have confined my references, as far as possible, to these texts themselves, and, very occasionally, to a few indispensable works of commentary and criticism. The historical settings in which I place my philosophers of peace and war are matters of common knowledge, if not of universally agreed interpretation, and it would have been pretentious to note the many different books from which they have been derived. Again, because the bibliographical literature, for each of my authors, is largely concerned with works that fall outside my purview, it would have been both clumsy and unsatisfactory to extract from it a selection of works or passages possessing some relevance to my chosen topic. I have, however, indicated where such bibliographical information can be found, except in the case of Tolstoy. My ignorance of Russian has confined me to the study of English translations of his major and finished works: a limitation which, I suppose, will be shared by most of my readers.

*Peterhouse, Cambridge*
*St Patrick's Day 1977*                                    W.B.G.

# I

# INTRODUCTORY

The chapters which follow deal with a handful of writers whose thoughts on peace and war have never, to my knowledge, been previously brought together for comparison, analysis and assessment. Except in one instance, their influences upon one another, although of interest, were not of the first importance. My authors form not a school, nor even a clear succession or progression of thought about peace and war; they form, rather, a constellation, a number of neighbouring sources of intellectual light converging upon, and suggesting the outlines of, the most urgent political problems of our age. As much by the differences in their approaches and conclusions as by the similarities and overlaps of their teachings, they help us to collect our thoughts, to begin to unify our still usually separate lines of thinking, about the roles and causes of war and the possibilities and conditions of peace between the peoples of the world: an enterprise which the ablest minds of previous ages had, with very few exceptions, either ignored or by-passed, and which researchers of our century, despite all their scientific and philosophical advantages, have done sadly little to advance.

Until the eighteenth century, international politics – centred on the use of the threat of war and expansion of commercial and cultural contacts – hardly admitted of systematic study: the contacts and conflicts of peoples and governments were too sporadic, variable and ill-recorded to admit of generalised description, still less of systematic prediction and control. But during the eighteenth century the future commercial unity of this globe was beginning to be recognised, as was the ever increasing cost of wars between the European powers – a cost that was to be measured not only by rising taxes but by the perpetual postponement of much needed constitutional reforms. This new situation was reflected, from different angles, in the writings of Montesquieu, Voltaire, Rousseau, and Vattel among others; but it was first expressed with philosophical authority and precision by Kant when he wrote in

1784 that 'the problem of establishing a perfect civil constitution is dependent on the  question of a law-governed relation between states, and cannot be solved until the latter is also solved'.[1] This statement, it is now natural to think, could and should have inaugurated a revolution in political philosophy; but nothing of the kind took place. On the contrary, while the next hundred and twenty years – roughly from the rise of Napoleon to the arrival of Lenin – saw many notable advances in the social sciences, in the specific field of political thought, and more specifically in the study of international relations, it showed a marked falling-off from the promise of the eighteenth century. And it is in the light of this falling-off that we most should ponder the judgement of Martin Wight, one of the few really notable 'international theorists' of our time, that 'international theory remains scattered, unsystematic, and mostly inaccessible to laymen. . .and marked not only by paucity but by intellectual and moral poverty'.[2]

In making this judgement, Martin Wight had in mind that established academic discipline, which seeks to achieve general truths and theoretical understanding of international relations on the basis, chiefly, of diplomatic history and international law. But while these two specialisms are no doubt indispensable for all detailed studies of international relations, one may doubt whether they can supply or evoke the historic vision and the mastery of categories required for understanding how our so-called international system has developed, and why it remains so profoundly unsatisfactory. The best contemporary work in international relations certainly tries to supply the required vision and categories; but progress in either direction has been piecemeal and has been retarded by the deep distrust which most historians feel for explanatory models of any kind. We can perhaps best come to appreciate the distinctive structure of the international problem, centred on the nature and causes of war and the possibilities of peace, by studying the reaction to it of a cluster of thinkers who were forced to face it at a time when it seemed very much simpler than we now know it to be. Kant, Clausewitz, Tolstoy and the founding fathers of Marxism all saw the international problem in what we today might well consider to be simplistic terms. But this does not mean that they showed themselves simpletons in their handling of it. On the contrary, I shall maintain, they identified certain of its most permanent elements with a clarity that could hardly be surpassed; and the more we appreciate their achievements in this respect, the better equipped we should be to deal with the new complexities of the international problems which have lately grown up around us.

My authors have another interesting feature in common. Each a supreme master in his particular field – Kant in philosophy, Clausewitz in military theory, the first Marxists in economics and the theory of revolution, Tolstoy in the novelistic presentation of both military and civilian life – found himself driven to engage with the international problem from his own peculiar viewpoint and in terms which reflect his own intellectual compulsions. This might suggest that my authors were a bunch of amateurs, and indeed amateurs whose separate endeavours could have little real bearing on each other's. The fact is, however, that their different approaches supplement each other to a remarkable degree. Indeed, the longer I have studied them, the more I have found myself regarding them as, almost, participants in a time-transcending dialogue. Nor is this at all absurd. For they were all men of immense intellectual force and range, deeply concerned with the plight of humanity, and in their different ways strangely prescient of the developing international scene. Their master-questions and their characteristic methods and approaches are, at first sight, wholly different; but the questions, methods and approaches of highly intelligent men always possess a wide range of relevance; and the main concern and conclusions of my authors constantly impinge on one another – now contradicting and challenging, now lending one another support in the most unexpected ways. Kant's answer to the characteristically philosophical question 'How are we to *conceive* the problem of peace?' might seem at first blush to have little connection with Clausewitz's struggle to pin down the element of rationality in war. But, as I shall argue, their arguments and conclusions, so differently motivated and so different in personal style and spirit, can be seen by us today to supplement one another to a degree which neither of their authors could possibly have appreciated. And similarly with my other authors: their thoughts and views, so bold and so passionately conflicting, so involved in the social and political struggles of their different times and places, are capable of yet further life if we are prepared to relive them as an inspiration and pro-paedeutic to our own intellectual endeavours. None of my authors ever met each other; and except for the Marxists' early recognition of Clausewitz, none of them showed much appreciation of the others' works. Yet, in bringing them together in these lectures, I am reasonably confident that I am not making either a historical, or a philosophical or, to indulge in a moment's whimsicality, even a social gaffe. If we can see the virtues of their different viewpoints on international matters, might not they themselves conceivably have done so? This is a line of thought to which I shall return in my concluding remarks.

3

In the chapters which immediately follow, however, I shall not be engaged simply in advertising and extolling the contributions of my authors to the understanding of international life. I have also before me a more humdrum, a harder, certainly an indispensably prior task: that of presenting their views on our topic in a fuller and clearer form, and in simpler terms, than they themselves succeeded in doing, or than most of their expositors have succeeded in doing since. A few words on the necessity of both these tasks will be useful here.

With the exception of Kant, all my authors were able, and some were of course outstandingly gifted, writers. Yet none of them produced a book, or even an essay, which does full justice to his concern with our topic. All Kant's political writings belong to his old age when his style was at its worst. Moreover Kant was one of the few philosophers in whom one *can* dissociate the style from the man: the former so obsessively pedantic, the latter, despite a few pathetic foibles, so heroically human. I have therefore felt no compunction about re-phrasing and reordering the views expressed in *Perpetual Peace* so as to bring out its most original probings, questions, arguments, and con-clusions – which Kant's clumsy efforts at popularisation in that pamphlet have served to conceal. With Clausewitz the difficulties are even greater. *On War* is an immensely impressive, almost a sublime book. But it was left unfinished, and contains some fundamental incon-sistencies, and many of its most important ideas are introduced in the most unexpected places, almost as marginalia or asides. Moreover, despite years of effort, Clausewitz never found a satisfactory way of expressing the central insight upon which most of his arguments hinge. His idea of Absolute War has never been adequately expounded, because it has never been adequately analysed and criticised with respect to its origins, to its place in Clausewitz's conceptual system, and to the confusions with which it is entangled in the opening chapter of his book. So Clausewitz, although his style has been compared for elegance with Goethe's and his best sayings belong to world-literature, stands in need of much sympathetic and critical reinterpretation, if he is to be genuinely appreciated. This may make parts of my chapter on Clausewitz difficult going; but I can only add that, in my belief, if the way is hard the prize is great. With Marx and his lieutenants the position is different again. None of them wrote anything that approximates to a treatise on international affairs, or on peace and war considered from a revolutionary socialist point of view. Their most perceptive, and also in some cases most self-betraying, utterances on our topic

4

are to be found in writings of the most varied kinds – popularisations of their central social doctrines, sketches of more specialised studies, political manifestos, newspaper articles, letters, scattered notes and memoranda. It is hardly surprising that these should show inconsistencies of which Marx, Engels, and Lenin seem to have been unaware. Recognition of such inconsistencies naturally passes into judgement on their importance, which is often difficult and always fallible. And I expect little thanks for my efforts in this regard from any party in the doctrinal struggle. Finally, what of Tolstoy? It might be imagined that, having inserted his general views on our topic in the body of one of the greatest and most popular novels ever written, he could hardly have failed to get them across to the public at large. But the result has been quite otherwise. Most readers of *War and Peace* have either skipped or skimmed through or fallen asleep over the philosophical disquisitions which it contains; while Tolstoy's later anti-war writings seem to have been taken seriously only by convinced pacifists (who, I suspect, must have found them curiously uncomforting) or by close students of the inner drama of his life and thought. Here again the fault lies largely with our author. Titan among writers though he was, Tolstoy lacked the skills of political persuasion, which, like Plato, he would not have deigned to cultivate. The result is that the wealth of general truths which one feels just below the living surface of *War and Peace*, and the (at least) brilliant half-truths which keep breaking through the dogma of his later 'Peace essays', have been almost wholly neglected by students of international relations.

But if, with all their gifts, my authors have failed to impress upon their readers their respective contributions to our topic, this failure has been aggravated by the persistent ineptitude, or excessively partisan spirit, of their expositors. This has been particularly true of Kant. Few of even his ablest expositors have taken his *Perpetual Peace* and related political writings seriously; while, with hardly an exception, those political and legal theorists who have been impressed by *Perpetual Peace*, have, as we shall find in Chapter 2, also been afflicted by something like word-blindness with respect to its actual arguments and conclusions. Indeed it is one of the greatest curiosities of political philosophy that the world had to wait till some fifteen odd years ago for a Cambridge scholar to construe the text and reconstruct the argument of Kant's pamphlet with the patience and care which its difficulties demand and the deftness of touch which its prodigious originality requires. Clausewitz has in some respects fared worse than Kant, having not only been bowdlerised by his first expositors – instructors in the military academies of nineteenth-century Prussia and France – but having had his text, in one crucial passage, deliberately falsified.[3] More recently, however, *On War* has been rewarded by a succession of scholarly treatments of high quality, notably those of the great Hans Delbrück and of Professor Raymond Aron, whose *Penser la guerre, Clausewitz* is as expectably impressive in its range and accuracy of treatment as it is moving in the generous sympathy of its spirit. Where Clausewitzian scholarship still falls short is in philosophical appreciation and criticism: neither the originality of Clausewitz's general philosophy of action nor the logical confusions involved in the doctrine of Absolute War have as yet received adequate attention from philosophers. With the Marxists, inevitably, differences over exposition and interpretation of key texts have usually been subordinated to differences over doctrinal orthodoxy on the one hand and scientific acceptability on the other. The result as regards our topic is that an important dimension of Marxist thought has remained virtually unstudied by Marxists and anti-Marxists, classical Marxists and neo-Marxists alike. I have therefore confined myself to the original sources of the Marxist contribution to international theory, which have retained their freshness largely because the doctrinal battles have passed them by. As to Tolstoy and his critics, I cannot speak so confidently, since the extensive criticism of *War and Peace* as history, which exists in Russian, is known to me only at second hand. I have the impression, however, that Tolstoy's critics have been much more interested in the biases and inaccuracies of his historical narrative and generalisations, and for that matter in his so-called philosophy of history, than in his much more central and passionate concern with what, in Chapter 5, I call 'the truth of war' – along with its endless falsities.

In sum, this book is primarily the examination of a number of texts concerned with a supremely important topic, and all contributing to it, in my belief, insights of lasting value. Considered severally, each of these texts deserves the careful study that is reserved, usually, for acknowledged masterpieces of science, history and imaginative literature. I have concentrated my attention on the compelling ideas, the *idées maîtresses*, behind these texts rather than on the brilliantly original personalities which they also serve to express. Nevertheless it is possible that I shall be accused of having over-personalised certain ideas whose importance consists in their permanent and impersonal relevance; and indeed, in so far as I compare and contrast my authors, I may have over-dramatised the logical relation between their different doctrines. But in a field of study whose practical implications are so great, and whose intellectual inspiration has until recently been so meagre, I feel that to over-personalise or over-dramatise the issues is a small fault, so long as it galvanises thought, quickens debate, and gives to future students the sense of having great allies behind them. The texts now to be studied may seem to have fallen and to have lain long on barren ground: but they have kept their vitality, and perhaps the ground is ready for their growth and flowering.

# KANT ON PERPETUAL PEACE

Kant's celebrated pamphlet, *Perpetual Peace*,[1] was published in Konigsberg, East Prussia, late in 1795. It is unique among Kant's writings in that it was written for a wide public, and that its publication can be regarded as a political act. It will be useful, therefore, to recall in outline the political situation which gave rise to it.

Prussia had taken a leading part in the war of intervention against the French revolutionary régime. But by the end of 1794 it had become clear that the French would not easily be conquered, and the Prussian government prepared to withdraw from the war, a decision which was ratified by the Treaty of Bâle, signed in January 1795. This event greatly impressed and delighted Kant; for although a political liberal, Kant was a dutiful citizen of autocratic Prussia; and although repudiating political rebellion (and still more regicide), he remained a passionate defender of the aims of the revolution. The new and more hopeful political climate encouraged him to make public his own revolutionary ideas of a revised international law, which he believed to be a necessary condition of any lasting peace. But not all the results of the Treaty of Bâle were to Kant's liking. Released from the war with France, Prussia joined in the third and final partition of Poland, an act which affronted Kant's principles and which he came as near to denouncing in his pamphlet as any Prussian citizen could have dared to do. Thus the possibility of great new political improvements and the threat of ever-recurrent political wickedness alike impelled him to speak out in a quite unusual way: not, as was his wont, in a scholastically worded, highly formalised treatise, but in a short, popular, strikingly direct and topical pamphlet. And judged by immediate results, Kant's attempt to give popular expression to his ideas seems to have worked well. The first edition of *Perpetual Peace* was sold out within a few weeks and a second edition, encumbered with two new philosophical appendices, which Kant could not forbear from adding, appeared early in the next year. Translations into English and French soon followed; and throughout the nineteenth century, particularly in English and American editions, the pamphlet continued to be read, and to be discussed in the literature of the peace movement. Indeed, during the early decades of our century *Perpetual Peace* was frequently cited – although far from correctly – as a notable precursor of the League of Nations idea.

But, judged by more stringent standards, Kant's attempt to make *Perpetual Peace* a popular work must be pronounced a failure, and indeed a disaster. It has tragically delayed a just appreciation of what Kant had to contribute to the understanding of international relations. He had no gift for lucid popular exposition; and it could hardly be expected that at the age of seventy, and after forty years devoted almost exclusively to abstract academic teaching and writing, he would at the first attempt produce an effective essay in political persuasion. And in fact his efforts at popularising his thoughts on European peace were to lead to a proliferation of contradictory interpretations which can hardly be matched in the history of political thought. Thus *Perpetual Peace* has usually been taken to be a call for immediate political action and to provide a recipe for the immediate achievement of a lasting European peace;[2] but it has also been interpreted as presenting a moral ideal to which states ought indeed to aspire in their external relations, although there is no chance of their actually attaining it.[3] Again it has been presented as a carefully qualified plea for the 'enforcement of peace' by the combined power of a league of peace-loving nations[4] – and with equal confidence, as a demonstration of the hopelessness of this policy. It has been widely taken to be a pacifist tract,[5] although in fact it expressly allows the creation of citizen militias for defence purposes.[6] And it has been hailed as a harbinger of world-government, despite Kant's clear rejection of this ideal and his insistence that his project leaves states with all their sovereign rights intact, apart from the right to make war at will.[7] Now to many minds it may seem that a work which admits of such conflicting interpretations cannot be of great importance. But before discussing this point, let me first try to give an introductory impression of the lay-out and the peculiar literary difficulties of Kant's pamphlet.

Its opening section is something of a *tour de force*. Without any preliminary discussion of why or in what circumstances war must be considered an unacceptable evil, Kant at once puts forward a number of 'Preliminary articles of Perpetual Peace between States'.[8] These are articles which, if honestly adhered to, might well have maintained peace between any eighteenth-century powers which agreed to them. They pledge the signatories to abjure all secret treaties; the acquisition of any state by another through inheritance, purchase or gift; the maintenance of standing armies; the incurring of a national debt for military purposes; any interference with the internal constitution of another state; and the use of assassins, subversion, etc. which make future peaceful relations between states virtually impossible. There can be little doubt that it is this first section, so forceful, and so straight-forward, which gained the pamphlet its immediate popularity and which also gave rise to the belief that in it Kant was offering the world a recipe for an immediate and lasting peace. Yet even in this opening section there are hints, especially in the footnotes, of a regression to the characteristic pedantries of Herr Doktor Professor Kant – a tendency which becomes more marked in the second section, which contains what Kant called the Definitive Articles of his treaty. By this he meant the main political presuppositions and safeguards without which no eighteenth-century state could seriously be expected to adhere to the earlier Definitive Articles.[9] In particular the signatories must enjoy what Kant calls a 'republican', i.e. in some degree a representative, constitution; their union or 'free federation' must be of the barest kind, confined to a repudiation of war-like or war-making acts against each other, while the enforcement of laws of common benefit to the signatories must be left to the *particular* state that is most immediately concerned. In this way Kant makes it clear that the signing of his preliminary articles would be only the *inauguration* of a long-term project of peace-building, whose completion would be a task calling for centuries of political experiment and effort in the face of recurrent disappointments, and which, even when accomplished, would never be perfectly secured. The section contains Kant's most original political thinking. But, notoriously, original thinking and popular exposition are not easily combined. And almost all popular expositions of *Perpetual Peace* are witnesses to the fact that Kant's purpose in his Definitive Articles has escaped the attention of most of his readers. With the third section, which contains his so-called Guarantee of Perpetual Peace, all pretence of popular exposition is abandoned. What we are given is not a guarantee in any known sense of the word, but at best a suggestion of how support for Kant's idea of perpetual peace may be found in his own (extremely subtle but here quite inadequately developed) philosophy of history. Finally, the two appendices which

Kant added to the second edition of *Perpetual Peace* are among the
most badly organised and over-abstract précis of philosophical argument that he ever perpetrated. So far, therefore, from being the effective
piece of popularisation which Kant had hoped to make it, *Perpetual
Peace* is a fantastic literary farrago, ranging in style from passages of
clarity and crispness to others in which, as Goethe remarked, Kant quite
out-Kants himself.

Let us now return, briefly, to Kant's expositors. It will be sufficient
to mention here one failing which, more than anthing else, helps to
explain their differences. Most of them wrote in the first half of our
century, and shared the characteristic political prejudices of their age.
In particular they have assumed that any serious advocate of peace,
such as Kant, must have worked out his ideas within limits set by some
or all of the following familiar dilemmas. He must *either* be an
advocate of 'peace-enforcement' by a league of peace-loving powers *or*
be a pacifist in the sense of renouncing the idea of national armed
defence. He must *either* be offering us a recipe for the institution of a
perpetual peace forthwith *or* be pointing to certain long-term trends
which, if duly followed and re-enforced, will (it is claimed) bring about
peace in the long run. More generally, he must rest his case *either* on a
moral appeal – always against the evils of war, but sometimes also
against violence of all kinds – *or* an appeal to enlightened self-interest
(usually involving faith in new international machinery which will
enable men and nations to live at peace without undergoing any drastic
moral transformation). Most of Kant's expositors, it seems to me, have
taken for granted that he must have accepted most, if not all, of these
dilemmas at the outset. But, as will become clear as we proceed, Kant
in fact accepted none of them. On the possibility of perpetual peace he
had a position which was as original and unique as it is difficult to
extract from the text of his pamphlet, and which indeed no one
succeeded in extracting completely, until Professor F. H. Hinsley did
so some fifteen years ago.[10] Moreover, since, as might be expected,
Kant's various expositors have favoured different alternatives within
the dilemmas just mentioned, it is not surprising that they should have
sought to enlist Kant's admittedly difficult teachings under so many
radically conflicting banners.

But when all explanations have been made, a natural doubt remains.
If Kant's central ideas in *Perpetual Peace* were of the same order as
those we find in other parts of his philosophy – in his theory of science,
in his refutation of metaphysics, in his foundations of ethics and law,

his philosophy of religion, even his aesthetics – then, one cannot but feel, no misfortune in their presentation would have been able to obscure them, no prejudices of their academic expositors could have accredited them with such a profusion of conflicting meanings. Now, as we shall find, Kant's thought in *Perpetual Peace* does betray important hesitations and inconsistencies, confusions and ambiguities. And it is also true that the movement of his thought, in all his political writings, suggests less the promptings of actual experience than a compulsion to rearrange the ideas of other thinkers, as if these were pieces in an (admittedly very important) jigsaw puzzle. Such weaknesses inevitably raise the question: had Kant anything of lasting importance to say about international relations – anything that was not already implicit in the enlightened commonsense of his own age or that is not taken for granted by students of international relations today? And that query might well seem to be supported by almost everything we know of Kant's life, circumstances and character.

His whole life had been spent in Prussia, an autocratic, militaristic state in which the middle classes enjoyed only a minimum of political rights. He taught and wrote, as a state-appointed professor in Prussia's smallest and poorest university, tucked away on its remote north-eastern frontier with Russia. Deprived of first-hand political experience, he was a voracious reader of foreign newspapers. But his knowledge of other countries was superficial, and his judgements on their politics were often priggishly obtuse. He had none of, for instance, Hegel's flair for detecting and analysing the growing-points of the politics of his day. His enthusiasm for the American, and still more for the French, revolutions was one of his most attractive traits, but it testified more to his generosity of spirit than to his political acumen. Nor were his obviously great intellectual gifts of the sort that we associate with political philosophy. With Kant, to think meant to schematise and to operate upon his schemata – to oppose, divide, combine and recombine them – in accordance with logical rules and the pull of his own deepest intuitions and compulsions. He is, *par excellence*, the philosopher of sharp antitheses and unbridgeable dichotomies. He had little interest in or sympathy with historical problems and methods. He seems to have been without interest in or admiration for the historian's characteristic gifts of passing from generalised narrative to explanations which, while logically incomplete, nevertheless suffice to direct the reader's attention into the appropriate channels, and of suggesting how influences and interests, commonly regarded as incompatible, may nevertheless have

been combined in a particular case. Not therefore, on the face of it, the
kind of philosopher from whom one would expect political ideas of an
original and revealing kind.

But here we should recall what very different kinds of enlightenment
different political philosophers have provided. Given the disadvantages
just listed, it would be absurd to expect from Kant the kind of contribution made by a Rousseau, a Hume or a Mill, all of whom, in their
different ways, had the capacity to raise current commentary on
political affairs to the level of philosophical reflection. From Kant we
would be wise to look for a contribution more ambitious if less effectively articulated, highly schematic but also directed with quite unusual
singleness of vision. And from this point of view, it may well be that
the restricted character of Kant's political experience was actually an
asset to him. From his Königsberg eyrie he had surveyed, beyond the
confines of his wretchedly suppressed Prussia, the politics of the
European cockpit. And if what he saw was a highly simplified, mono-
chrome vision, at least he saw it clearly and saw that it was bad. For
Frederick's Prussia was only an extreme example of what was basically
the common situation of all the dynastic states of eighteenth-century
Europe. Even in those which appeared to be most progressive, war and
the continued preparation for war were the main preoccupation of
governments, delaying when they did not altogether forbid the prospects of constitutional reform. But Prussia was Kant's own state, and its
combination of persistent constitutional backwardness with equally
persistent aggression against its neighbours had pained and shamed him
acutely. It had also enabled Kant, however, to formulate strong and
clear views of the relation between arbitrary government at home and
aggressive policies abroad. And he had given some indication of these
in his *Ideas for a Universal History* published ten years before
*Perpetual Peace.* There he had made the claim, which we have already
cited, that 'the problem of establishing a perfect civil constitution is
dependent upon the problem of a law-governed relationship between
states'. With this claim, which Kant might well have used as a proem
to *Perpetual Peace*, he had already taken a revolutionary step forward
in political philosophy, although in a direction in which, until quite
recently, he had virtually no followers. He had made the first significant
attempt – its success is a question we shall try to decide – to construct a
framework of ideas within which the generally acknowledged rights
and duties of states *vis-à-vis* their *own* citizens can be shown to require,
logically, acknowledgement of certain equally important rights and

duties towards each other (and each other's citizens) if their traditionally recognised tasks are ever to be effectively discharged. And it is as
part of this framework of ideas – of the new meaning Kant gives to the
idea of international law – that his demand for perpetual peace must
be understood.

This is Kant's most obviously original slant on, and approach to,
political philosophy. And had he developed it adequately it might well
have been regarded as yet another of the Copernican Revolutions which
he introduced into philosophy. And yet it is not the only original,
perhaps not the most original, feature of Kant's political thinking; a
second, which springs from the central tensions of his whole intellectual
system, can be described here only in the barest outline.

Among the sharp and rigid dichotomies of his system, Kant's treatment of Reason stands out for its surprising flexibility and imaginative
power. Formally, the idea of Reason functions as an undefined constant
in that system – as an idea so basic as to defy definition. But, as Kant
explores the main regions of human experience, his idea of Reason
takes on a character which, although continuous with the rather com-
posite character accorded to it in the history of philosophy, yet shows a
coherence and a dynamism never disclosed in any previous system of
thought. To speak very roughly, Kant presents Reason as that tendency, in all human thought and conscious effort, towards, at one and
the same time, ever greater unity, system and necessity, and *equally*
towards ever sharper and more constant self-criticism and self-control.
The former aspect of Reason is more evident in its task of ordering our
subjective sense-impressions into our knowledge of an objective, public,
law-governed physical world; the latter in its task of subjecting our
egoistic impulses to rules of consistency, reciprocity and fairness; but
'one and the same Reason', as Kant was wont to say, finds expression
alike in theoretical and in practical life. On the other hand, Reason
appeared to have met with very unequal success in these two spheres.
Considered as vehicles of Reason's quest for unity, system and necessity,
men for the most part have easily reached agreement about how objects
in their common world should be identified, related and explained.
But they have been far less successful, Kant believed, in reaching agreement – or at least in acting in accordance with agreed rules – on
questions of reciprocity and fairness between man and man. Consequently Kant was driven, early in his career, into something very close
to the intellectualist 'ivory tower' view that human Theoretical Reason
'works' – in particular it gives us science – whereas human Practical

Reason, conceived as a system of rules restraining human egoism, does not: and that in particular the task of administering and enforcing public rules which is politics has largely been a sorry history of misrule at home and of vicious anarchy in international relations.

From this ivory tower attitude Kant tells us that he was rescued by reading Rousseau, who taught him to see that mankind's highest intellectual achievements were as nothing when compared with even the most modest of its achievements in the moral and political sphere. But even when Kant had assimilated this lesson into his general philosophy, his conception of the two main functions of Reason – theoretical and practical – left him facing enormous difficulties. These were due, largely, to his acceptance of Newtonian physics as the paradigm of all theoretical knowledge. Theoretical Reason, it seemed to him, demanded and disclosed a world of natural determinism – confirmed in that necessary order of our sensations which can be construed as an ordered, public, material world. Practical Reason, on the other hand, demanded or presupposed the possibility of human freedom to choose what Duty or Justice commands, despite the determination, by physical and psychological causes, of all our everyday actions. It is this antithesis which, more than anything else, gives Kant's philosophy its characteristic strength, even if that strength sometimes borders on perversity. Theoretical Reason demands a completed system; Practical Reason an ever-open, never-completed task or calling. Or, to put the antithesis in another way, the chasm which Kant had set between Natural Necessity (the object of Theoretical Reason) and Human Freedom (the presupposition of Practical Reason) could never be bridged, still less denied. Yet the dominant tendency of Kant's philosophical thought during the 1790s – the period of his most intense preoccupation with politics – was to explore areas in which it was at least possible that these antithetical aspects of the world, equally required by Reason, could be conceived to be contributing to a common end. Kant first examined this possibility in connection with the ostensible teleology of living forms; and from here he transferred his somewhat tentative ideas to the history of mankind's political endeavours and misfortunes. Might not this be construed as a succession of naturally necessitated misadventures, spiced with episodes of ostensible good luck, through which men could nevertheless learn, by trial and error, to expand the area of their own rational freedom? More specifically, might it not be that the characteristic difficulties, failures and tragedies disclosed in the history of mankind, constituted a necessary condition for the expansion of men's capacity to cope rationally with nature's challenges, and to begin to co-operate in the face of them? The ultimate goal of such rational progress would be a world of lasting peace between nations, a blessing which would at once support and be supported by their enjoyment of what we should call liberal-democratic institutions at home.

The intensity of feeling which Kant focused upon this hope for Reason in human life is unparalleled in the history of political thought, anyhow since Plato. It seemed to him that the worthwhileness of the whole 'human experiment' depended, not indeed upon proof of that hope – something as impossible, for Kant, as proofs of the existence of God, freedom or immortality – but upon a sense of its genuine openness, as the necessary context of men's political aspirations and endeavours. Contrary to the common criticism (first put about by Hegel), that Kant's moral philosophy was meanly centred on the individual's concern with his own private virtues, the idea that the worth of any individual life can be gauged only on a scale that involves reference to all human life, had been present in Kant's thought since its early pre-Critical days. And now the question of what the unity of mankind, as a moral idea, consists in; of how it relates to the idea of mankind's worth and destiny; and of what it means for a man to act as a member and representative of the human race, began to fuse in his thought with the newer more specific hopes, raised by the French Revolution and by what Kant believed (somewhat over-optimistically) to have been the characteristic reception of the Revolution by men of good will in all European countries. This strange upsurge of moral and intellectual enthusiasm, and the almost parentally anxious hope for humanity that accompanied it, enabled Kant to adumbrate a political attitude which is perhaps even more pertinent to the world of today than it was when he struggled to express it, in a race against time and failing powers, some hundred and eighty years ago. The political writings of Kant's last years may give the impression of an old man in a hurry, trying to grapple with problems he was never completely at home with, and for dealing with which his own portentous philosophical machinery gave him very little assistance. Yet the overall effect of these writings is profoundly moving; for the old man in a hurry was one who, after a lifetime given to the pursuit of ideas, now believed that his ideas had landed him at last at the heart of human life, at one of the unique moments and growing-points in human history, which it was is duty to explicate and defend, from the widest of all possible viewpoints, that of Reason, and yet in language which ordinary men could understand.

Kant, then, had cause, motive, inspiration and intellectual vitality enough to embark, however belatedly and however imperfectly equipped, on his original course in political philosophy. This is more than enough to justify the most strenuous and sympathetic study of it, no matter how great and at times how irritating the attendant difficulties may be. And during the last two decades, his political thought, particularly as found in *Perpetual Peace*, has begun to receive the kind of attention that it deserves and requires. In two vital respects the arguments and conclusions of *Perpetual Peace* have now been clarified, if not quite fully and finally, at least to the point where the experience of reading it has been transformed. First, when Kant's pamphlet is read in the light of its predecessors – the treatises of St Pierre and Rousseau on one side and of Vattel on the other – many of the oddities in its structure and argument quickly become intelligible. In his *Power and the Pursuit of Peace* Professor F. H. Hinsley has revealed Kant as – in his theory of international relations – largely the corrector of Rousseau, whom he loved and revered; and in later studies Hinsley has also shown how great a stimulus Kant derived from the writings of Vattel, whom he so unjustly disparaged and despised. And it is astonishing how much easier it is to see what Kant is arguing *for*, when one knows exactly whom he is arguing *against*. But secondly, Hinsley and, in a lesser degree, Hemleben, Waltz, Gay and others have skilfully revealed the main structural links, and the main gaps and ambiguities, within the positive argument of *Perpetual Peace* itself; indeed I would say that there is now no main thesis or argument, or caustic aside, in this work that has not been given its proper place and weight within Kant's total design. Yet despite this outstanding scholarly work by recent historians – so different from the neglect shown by most Kantian specialists – something still seems to me to be lacking. It is as if, while careful judgments are converging on almost every particular difficulty in Kant's pamphlet, the distinctive physiognomic unity of its teaching – the central aim and message of its often straggling or truncated arguments – has still to be adequately realised and conveyed. And for this reason I now propose to set out in my own words, free from every trace of Kantese, first and quite briefly, what I take to have been his main debt to his predecessors in our field, and secondly and more fully, what I believe to have been his main positive intentions in writing *Perpetual Peace*.

Kant, like Rousseau and Vatel before him, wrote of international relations almost entirely in terms of the eighteenth-century European scene. This conformed to the age-old view of the life of men and nations as an endless alternation between war and peace (conceived as little more than a temporary cessation of war) from which there appeared to be no possible escape. Most eighteenth-century political theorists, however, believed that Europe, as they knew it, differed from most if not all previous state-systems in two important respects. First, all European states were agreed to be the heirs of a great common civilisation (described by some as classical, by others as Christian), and equally to be the likely participators in a great common future, artistic, scientific and commercial. Secondly, it was widely believed that, although wars continued to rage almost incessantly, their greatest threat to civilisation – the overthrow and destruction of established political units within natural borders – was now considerably mitigated by a principle of equilibrium inherent in the eighteenth-century state-system. This principle ensured that, whenever an ambitious European power threatened to conquer and absorb its neighbours, its actions would eventually produce an alliance of other powers to resist it, since a serious threat to any one state (by the ambitious, rising power) could quickly develop into a threat to all. War, therefore, was not simply a necessary evil within the European system, it was also an indispensable safeguard of the survival and independence of the different European states. And as such, in spite of its destructiveness and wastefulness, it was a fact of life which men must continue to tolerate.

Both Rousseau (here following St Pierre) and Vattel were dissatisfied with this over-complacent picture; in particular, despite other sharp differences, both rightly distrusted its assumption of a permanent equilibrium between the main European states, maintained by the use or threat of war. Contrary to most of his contemporaries, Rousseau argued that war between the European states was an inherently ever-increasing evil; that it was the main obstacle to the progress of domestic reforms; that Reason demanded its elimination, and that this could be achieved – without the tyranny involved in all great empires – only by the formation of a strong federation of European states. However, he then tempered this conclusion by admitting that he saw no possibility of the different European states submitting to effective federal rule; so that, in effect, he abandoned the international problem as insoluble.[11] Vattel's position was at first sight much more positive and practical.[12] He agreed with Rousseau that war was at once inherent in the

European state-system and a grave obstacle to the advance of its commercial and cultural development. The best one could do with war, however, was to limit or moderate it. But this required that men and states first recognised war's true character and the results that can reasonably be expected from it. To begin from the latter point: the less destructive a war, and the less vindictive the peace terms imposed by the victor, the longer and more secure the resulting peace could be expected to be; and a secure, advantageous and relatively lasting peace is the only rational aim in any war. But, Vattel insisted, moderation in war and at the peace-table required that men should first discard the idea that some wars, or some party in every war, are peculiarly 'just', or that either side in any war is ever entitled to regard its action as 'punitive' in the legal sense. On the contrary, every sovereign state having the right to make war for what it regards as its own interests, all wars – and both sides in every war – are equally just. Victory and defeat are purely factual matters, the results of a quite arbitrary (irrational) method of settling those differences between states which defy the rational methods of bargaining and arbitration. We must, however, accept *some* method of settling such differences. And at a sensible peace-settlement, victor and vanquished begin by recognising the new state of the facts, brought about by the war; and in the light of this – and not of sham-judicial claims – they then strike the best bargain possible, one which evidently favours the victor, but not to such an extent as to drive the vanquished to repudiate it at the first opportunity. In sum, therefore, war was, for Vattel, an inescapable fact and tool of political life, but one which governments should be persuaded to use with ever greater moderation, ever more rarely, although not in the credulous hope that it could be entirely dispensed with.

In his international theory Kant owed less to Rousseau (apart from personal inspiration) than he imagined, and more to Vattel than he was ready to admit. He agreed with Rousseau that war was an intolerable evil, and that steps ought to be taken forthwith towards ending the use of war by states for the enforcement of what they took to be their rights; and he agreed again with Rousseau that the establishment of a strong European federation, even if theoretically capable of putting an end to wars between its members, was a practical impossibility. But he also came to see that Rousseau had hoped for too easy and too immediate a solution for so deep-rooted a political evil as war. Kant agreed with Vattel on one all-important point; namely, that nothing but confusion and harm resulted from regarding *any* wars as just or punitive – war in itself being inherently 'anti-law', even when inescapable, and certainly no way for rational men to try to secure their rights. He was also in something like agreement with Vattel in recognising that the task of coping with the evil of war would inevitably be a long, slow and arduous one. On the other hand he bitterly repudiated Vattel's concession that all states have a right to go to war to secure what they take to be their interests, and his consequent claim that the best one can do about war is to moderate and limit it, without hoping vainly to eliminate it from the international scene. As against this, Kant was to maintain that recognition of the aim of perpetual peace between nations was necessary as a first step in any assured progress towards a lawful international order, and consequently that to believe in the possibility of a progressive moderation and limitation of wars, without acceptance of that aim, was a most dangerous delusion.

So much, in very rough outline, for what Kant accepted, and just as significantly what he rejected, in the teachings of his two great predecessors. We are now in a position to appreciate the entirely new – indeed revolutionary – conception of international law which Kant was to create from those elements in Rousseau's and Vattel's views with which he agreed, combining them in such a way, however, that the aspects of their theories with which he disagreed disappear completely from the picture. The resulting conception was far too original to be fully appreciated when Kant first gave it to the world. It is only in the last four decades that its boldness, its moderation, its apparent practicality and at the very least its permanent pertinence to international problems, have become plain. Here, by way of signposts to the exposition which follows, are what seem to me to be its four most salient features.

First, Kant was not a pacifist, but rather a passionate *legaliser*, or prophet or evangelist of progressive legalisations, in international relations. Secondly, despite his constant emphasis on the necessity of coercion to sustain the law within any established state, he was equally emphatic that the idea of coercion, to sustain an international order, is both logically and practically an absurdity. An international order could be initiated only when certain governments freely abjured their right to make war on each other; and it would expand only as other governments, observing the benefits (in the way of greater economy and security) which accrued from this initiative, sought membership within the bond (*foedus*) of mutual non-aggression. Thirdly, Kant believed – paradoxically, and some might think fanatically – that in order to work, an international order must be confined to the one paramount task of keeping the peace between such like-minded states as chose to sign a non-aggression treaty (on the lines of his suggested Preliminary Articles). Complete non-interference in the internal affairs of every signatory state seemed to him an essential precondition of faithful adherence, by any sovereign state, to the treaty which he proposed. Kant, the first systematic internationalist, was thus also one of the most steadfast of 'statists' in the history of political thought. Fourthly, Kant saw the task of creating a world-wide international order within a very long historical perspective. It would be a task subject to all manner of attacks, set-backs, and disappointments. But these could be lightened by two considerations. Kant was convinced that there was no other way forward, in international relations, than the one which he presented. In following it, therefore, men could be assured that they were doing all that is possible towards the fulfilment of their cosmopolitan duty and calling. And more generally, men should always remember that, as a species, they are distinguished by their capacity to learn by trial and error and by a sense of their ideal goal – to live justly and in harmony with one another. Here as elsewhere, therefore, we must do what we see to be right, hoping that even our errors, failures and disappointments may be of service in the long run.

## Kant's Legalism

Although not a pacifist, Kant regarded war as the greatest evil besetting human societies, and in one passage he goes so far as to describe war as the source of all evils and of all moral corruption.[13] But he did not see war as an evil which admits of any one complete and immediate cure. It was the extreme form of the general evil – the natural egoism – in human nature which had, first, to be tamed by the enforcement of laws, no matter how harsh and imperfectly rational, and which only thereafter could be directed towards the political ideal of lawful freedom, within which pure social morality – men treating each other as ends, never as means – would be at least partially realised. But while insisting on the inherent evil of war, Kant acknowledges that every citizen should be prepared to defend his country from foreign invasion.[14] Indeed he seems to have regarded self-defence (at the national as much as at the personal level) as a natural reaction, essential in life. As such it is admissible, although in no way contributing to the cause of international justice. On the other hand it is the voluntary decision of one government to attack another which Kant identifies – and condemns as wholly unjust or wildly 'anti-law' – as war.

The strength of Kant's legalist attitude, which thus far echoes his account of the citizen's allegiance to the state, is that, for him, genuinely to value anything, for instance to value a human personality or any basic human right, entails committing oneself to secure, for that person or right, a *legally protected status*, so far as one's circumstances and other commitments allow.[15] This commitment requires, before anything else, that men shall form political societies – states – and shall obey the laws that are enforced within their own particular state by its generally recognised government. Kant's view of men's political allegiance to their own state could well be described as petrified Rousseau; it is spare, bleak and unbending to a degree that none of us today would find acceptable. But it has the merit of insisting on two points which, although they are quite compatible, few recent political philosophers have cared – or dared – to emphasise together. These are, first, that a sincere demand for the rule of law entails acceptance of irresistible power in the hands of government, and on the other hand, that the existence of effective government requires that most of its subjects, most of the time, obey its laws *because they think it right to do so*, not because they find law-keeping is to their private advantage. Kant of course had in mind governments whose tasks – mainly of a protective and punitive character – were easily recognised and relatively fixed, and were indeed minimal in comparison with what almost all people expect from government today. Nevertheless, and to a greater degree than is usually admitted, Kant recognised that new tasks of government are always liable to arise as circumstances, needs and the level of public enlightenment change. And among such political changes, one of paramount importance seemed to him to have emerged in eighteenth-century Europe and to have become an urgent duty upon all European governments. This was the task of replacing their natural lawlessness (or their condition of chronic war or readiness-for-war with each other) by a legal relationship in which their differences would be settled by mediation and arbitration rather than by armed force.

But recognition of the second great task of government had not been due to any sudden moral illumination: its necessity and urgency had been brought home to even cynically self-centred minds by a number of historical developments – the rise of sovereign nation states, the increased efficiency of state administrations since the mid-seventeenth century, and the ever-rising cost of wars waged by standing armies.

In this situation it was natural for men to look askance at the European nations engaged in almost constant war with one another, and to turn with interest to projects for a lasting European peace. Kant's project differed from all others which had preceded it in that it combined an urgent moral demand for 'action now' with a politically sagacious recognition of the long uphill struggle which that action would require. Governments, he argued, had an immediate duty to *inaugurate* peace,[16] in the form of an embryonic legal order, intended to be perpetual, and thereafter gradually to extend it until, ultimately, it covered the globe. Only as thus conceived could the age-old longing of mankind for peace here, now, everywhere and for ever, be given a coherent, practically feasible as well as a morally compelling form. But peace-intended-to-be-perpetual could not be inaugurated without a revision of mankind's conception of international law. Its inauguration would therefore be a real beginning, a creative and revolutionary change in legal as much as in political history. Thus Kant's 'legalist' approach to politics, which had such grimly restrictive effects on his treatment of the citizen's allegiance to his state, was to prove a liberating force in the field of foreign relations.

## Legalism and coercion

Publicists, philosophers and sometimes governments have sought an escape from constant war by either of two means: by imagining or creating vast empires within which all hostilities have been beaten down, or by imagining or engaging in strong federations of independent sovereign states, united only for mutual defence and for such common services as mutual defence requires. The latter alternative was of particular interest to Kant since it had recently been readvertised (although with ultimate doubt and faint-heartedness) by his hero Rousseau; but Kant rejected it as firmly as he rejected the suggestion of peace-through-empire.[17] Vast empires do not solve the problem of inter-state relations, they merely replace it by a situation of large-scale tyranny within which, by definition, specifically inter-state conflicts do not arise. Now, from the point of view of attaining a permanent peace this new situation is no real improvement on the old one. For large empires cannot command deeply based loyalty and support, and invariably break down into component warring groups for which the problem of creating a legal order will arise exactly as before. Subjection to a vast empire is in fact a condition further removed from what international justice requires than is the characteristic anarchy of sovereign states. The latter condition at least points to an urgent problem; the former deludes men into thinking they have solved it. The second suggested approach through a federation of free states, looks more promising, but turns out to be equally delusive. Any government that genuinely subscribes to the creation of a combined force, capable of imposing peace within the federation, will *eo ipso* be putting itself out of business – the last thing that any government can be expected to do. For, if the federation is strong enough to enforce peace, it will become in fact a super-state, inevitably overriding the rights of its members. On the other hand, if the federation is not strong enough to do this, the inevitable rivalries of its members will pull them back into international anarchy.

Kant's rejection of both these positions puts him into a difficulty. For what they most obviously have in common is their reliance upon coercion to maintain a lasting peace between human societies; and Kant could not have been more emphatic in insisting that what he called 'lawful, public coercion' was needed to secure basic freedoms *within* any particular political society. This being so, it would have seemed natural for him to insist, even more emphatically, on the necessity of lawful coercion of some kind to establish and maintain an effective legal relation between independent, and for the most part hitherto warring, states. But he did not. The impracticability of projects of peace-by-empire and of peace-by-federation had persuaded him that the idea of enforcing peace between sovereign states was a sheer political delusion. In this respect, Kant had come to believe, there is a fundamental asymmetry between establishing and maintaining a just constitution within a state and in establishing and maintaining a just relationship between states. This does not mean that there is no place for force in inter-state relations. On the contrary, Kant recognised that until his proposed legal order included all states, there would always be calls for the use of force in self-defence against lawless aggressors.[18] But, it is an essential part of Kant's position that such uses of force, even if they be supported by other peace-loving allies, do nothing, positively and specifically, to advance the cause of perpetual peace. An act of defensive war may be justified as preserving a (relatively) just state in existence; but it cannot be justified in respect of that kind of relation between states which Reason positively requires that all states should strive to bring into being.

## Confederation, but for what?

Kant's positive proposal is that states should form a confederation for a strictly limited purpose. His alternative descriptions for what he has in mind are, 'federative association', 'partnership or confederation' and 'permanent congress of states'.[19] But what does Kant's confederation bind its members to do – and not to do?

Here his view varies, and varies much more than he himself can have realised, in his different writings on peace. In *Perpetual Peace* the primary aim is, quite explicitly and unquestionably, the ending of all aggression *between such powers as would sign his treaty of permanent mutual non-aggression*. But in other important writings, some earlier and some later than *Perpetual Peace*, which deal with international law and the prospects of peace, Kant wrote as if the above 'primary' aim was rather to be considered as the by-product of something very different, viz. a confederation for common defence against aggression, by outsiders, against the signatory powers. On the former view the primary aim was peace *between* the signatories; on this second view it appears to be to secure peace for the signatories – *from aggression by other parties.*

To many of Kant's twentieth-century expositors a simple way of reconciling these outwardly very different approaches to peace was as follows. The second view (possibly foreshadowed in *The Idea of a Universal History* of 1784 and almost certainly intended in part I of the *Metaphysics of Morals* of 1797) discloses the 'teeth' of the proposed confederation, the secret of its political efficacy and power of growth; whereas the former view, although true, expresses what is virtually a truth by definition. For unless the confederates remain at peace with one another, how can they effectively resist and progressively beat back aggressive outsiders? But in fact Kant nowhere develops this second way of thinking, and there is not a trace of it in *Perpetual Peace*, the one work in which Kant is directly and exclusively concerned with our topic. The real strength – if not the 'teeth' – of his proposed federation lies in its capacity to maintain and extend peace among a number of like-minded powers. In this way it will demonstrate both that arbitration is the only morally acceptable way in which states can secure their rights, and that marked non-aggression *pays* – in a quite material sense – in a world where war is becoming ever more costly and more destructive. This position certainly allows that any of Kant's signatory powers may have to engage in joint defensive action against aggressors, and should maintain citizen militias to meet the danger of invasion. But such action, although justified in what Kant calls a 'provisional' sense, does not contribute in any direct way to the cause of perpetual peace, which it is now the clear duty of all governments to establish and extend.

A number of Kant's teachings – whether in the form of maxims, arguments or criticisms – make it abundantly clear that, for him, peace-intended-to-be-perpetual is something that must spread from a positive example of pledged non-aggression, successfully sustained in the first instance by a few like-minded states. First, there is his strenuous denunciation of those early international lawyers, Grotius, Puffendorf and most particularly Vattel, who had sought to persuade European states to content themselves with strictly limited wars, as a necessary condition of peace-settlements that could be expected to endure. Kant will have none of this insidiously 'comforting' approach to the problem of peace;[20] and not, as one might expect, because of the great difficulty of keeping any war within proposed limits once it has begun, but because, in Kant's reconstructed international law, everything depends upon – and also points towards – the thought that 'war is no way in which to pursue one's rights', since it amounts to the irrational acceptance of the rule of the stronger, and is an affront to Reason's demand that interstate relations shall be put on a legal footing. When this is the governing principle, it is clear that a peace voluntarily sought and sustained by both or all sides is a much better starting-point than a peace which depends on the power of a defensive alliance to beat back aggressors – who may well not accept the lesson of defeat. This argument is given further support by a point which Kant makes very forcibly in part I of his *Metaphysics of Morals*. If an effective defensive alliance were the core of his proposals, it would be difficult to deny his confederates the rights (a) to force other powers to join them, and (b) to force any of their members that wanted to secede to remain within the alliance. But Kant was strongly inclined to deny the first of these rights to his confederation and he expressly denies the second;[21] since both would mean an infringement of the sovereign rights of states, and both would lead from the paradoxical attempt to enforce peace to the self-contradictory attempt to maintain or strengthen peace-keeping machinery by threatening or engaging in war.

Equally impressive, from this point of view, is Kant's account of what effective international law would require of its adherents, over and above their decision to abandon war for arbitration in the settlement of their disputes. For this makes it clear that his vision of perpetual peace is not of a world kept at peace by a central confederate power, but of a world in which every state manifests its own independence in fulfilling the *one* job of enforcement which Kant's conception of international law requires.[22] Kant looks forward to a world in which it would be legally permissible for any citizens of any state to visit the territory of any other state with a view to doing business there. But if the form or the results of such business should turn out to offend the laws of the visited state, then the visitors would be constrained to leave: and it would be the duty of the host state to see to it that the visitors did leave – and leave, if possible, unharmed and alive. (We must remember that among the visitors Kant had in mind were would-be colonisers and would-be slave-traders as well as those engaged in commendable commercial and cultural exchanges.) Thus for Kant, as much as for Adam Smith and his disciples, free movement of men and goods was an essential facet of a peaceful and civilised world: but subject always to the laws and the powers of enforcement of *existing states*. His cosmopolitan ideal is, therefore, neither a world-state, as so many of his expositors have so inexcusably maintained, nor an anarchistic Utopia in which states have been dispensed with. It is, rather, the hope or promise of a world in which the individual's rights come to transcend the boundaries of his own nation, being secured – and of course also limited – not by any supernational authority, but by the mutual recognition, among the confederate states, of their rights and duties *vis-à-vis* each other's nationals. This has nothing to do with pledges or plans of mutual alliance for defence or for the enforcement of peace. It is rather a first step towards ensuring positively pacific relations between such independent states as show a respect for law at home and abroad.

## What guarantee of perpetual peace?

Kant's repeated insistence that his proposed confederation would not be an 'international state', that it would leave its members as sovereign as before, and that it expressly excludes the idea of peace-enforcement (particularly with regard to would-be seceders from its membership), naturally gives rise to the question: but what else, over and above their recognition of the moral unacceptability of war, will hold its members together when, inevitably, differences, rivalries and suspicions arise between them? This brings us to Kant's so-called guarantee of perpetual peace, which has two very surprising features. First, as Kant makes clear in a number of passages, he is not offering a foolproof guarantee that his confederation will not break down – and incidentally he offers *no* guarantee that it may not be overwhelmed at the outset by militaristic powers which detest any idea or project for perpetual peace. On the contrary, a most important part of Kant's idea is that such assurance of success for his confederation as can be offered must depend, at all stages of its development, upon the *persistently remembered possibility, if not the actual danger or threat*, of its members lapsing back into the habit of irresponsible war. We shall return to this point – which of course recurs in modern theories of deterrence – in a few moments. But secondly – and this is something which Kant fails to bring out – his so-called guarantee would have been far better described as, or at least introduced as, a rebuttal of the natural objection that his confederation, being aimed at the gradual and difficult expansion of peace, is bound to collapse, given the ineradicable and overpowering egoism, meanness, deceitfulness and distrustfulness of human nature. His guarantee is in fact an almost exact equivalent, in his political thinking, to his 'defences' – *not* proofs – of the ideas of God, freedom and immortality in his metaphysical (or, if it be preferred, his anti-metaphysical) writings. Kant argued there that the necessary limitations of human knowledge rendered a proof of the reality of, for example, freedom impossible, but equally ruled out any possible disproof of its existence; and on this basis he went on to claim that if (and indeed since) certain moral demands compel us to act as if we were always free to choose rightly, therefore we are entitled to believe that (though we can never *know* or understand *how*) we possess moral freedom. Similarly with his ill-named 'guarantee' of perpetual peace. It is Kant's way of urging, against those who find in human nature certain immovable barriers to political progress, that these barriers can always also be regarded as necessary challenges or springboards to rational human effort; and that this way of regarding them is in fact the only way in which we can make sense of what little we know of mankind's political development.

To put this last point more positively, Kant accepts the traditional view of man as in part animal and inherently egoistic, in part rational and law-respecting. The latter – rational – capacities, although capable of only limited development in each individual, have nevertheless almost unlimited possibilities of development within the species as a whole. But they can only be called into action through the needs and promptings of our animal nature, which is far from ideally adapted to its environment, and which constantly brings the species into danger of self-destruction. It is the perils, the crises, the agonies and the anomalies of human life which arouse naturally idle and habit-bound mankind to the ingenuity and inventiveness, the clear-sightedness and respect for justice, which are the hall-marks of human rationality.[23] But abstract awareness of the injustice of war, for example, or of war's main causes, or of the main means by which these causes might be diverted or forestalled, will never be sufficient to produce peace between nations. The rational human will, as Kant bitterly observed, is as admirable in itself as it is impotent in practice.[24] Only as war becomes patently more destructive and more costly, will men be moved to take the first difficult steps towards a permanent peace. The general character of these steps seemed to Kant to be perfectly plain: there was no difficulty in seeing what must be attempted, and what foregone, if a peace intended to be perpetual is to be inaugurated. (Acceptance of his Preliminary Articles by two or three powers would give the project a start). But Kant fully recognised that the task of bringing the different nations of mankind to make the necessary initiatives and concessions, and to sustain them, would be a long and arduous one, would be one of the last problems to be solved by the human race.[25] And even when it may appear to be solved – that is, when Kant's free confederation comes to embrace all existing states and nations – there would always remain the possibility of misunderstandings and backslidings into ruthless, irresponsible egoism and war. And yet, paradoxically, it is only the recognition of this persistent danger that can sustain Reason's demand that states' rights must be secured by legal means, which necessarily excludes the use of war.

Such, then, is the fundamental structure of Kant's international thought. Let us now attempt a brief assessment of it, beginning with its most obvious gaps, weaknesses, waverings and uncertainties.

First among the latter I would put the narrowness, the provincialism in time and place, of the general political outlook which it expresses. Kant writes as if all wars were struggles for local advantage between eighteenth-century European states, motivated by the greed of governments rather than of peoples. It is as if Kant had never heard of mass invasions, of wars of whole peoples or cities, driven to exterminate or enslave one another by economic, demographic, religious or ethnic causes. Again he makes no mention of social or civil wars, although he does write, with undisguised distaste, of the wars of colonial conquest fought by European powers in the less developed parts of the world. And he is equally blind to the ways in which wars, by providing an excuse for armies, have served to secure many régimes from popular revolt. In fine, wars for Kant are always a matter of morally bad governments ordering their troops to attack, and occupy the lands of, their morally indifferent foes – who would probably have engaged in similar aggression if they had had the chance. This first weakness in Kant's treatment of our topic is undeniable. To admit it means recognising that the problems of inaugurating and extending peaceful relations between states is a much more complicated business than a quick reading of *Perpetual Peace* might lead one to believe. On the other hand, it should be remembered that Kant insists, again and again, upon the difficulties, the disappointments, the uphill efforts, and above all the time, which his project of perpetual peace must inevitably involve.

Secondly, while allowing that wars of self-defence against aggression must be condoned until such time as his federation embraces all nations, Kant makes no distinction between wars of a moderate or limited character, such as might well result in an acceptable and lasting peace, and wars of outrage which either pass into massacre and enslavement or give rise to endless international blood-feuds. In Kant's view, all wars alike stand condemned by Reason for their manifest anti-legality. Here he may well seem wooden, dogmatic and unrealistic when compared with Vattel, who argued so persuasively for limited wars, at the end of which relatively lasting settlements could be expected. It should be remembered, however, that Kant was proposing perpetual peace, first between a few like-minded nations and only ultimately between all nations, as a new political ideal, comparable in importance to recent declarations of the Rights of Man. It is in this light that his unqualified condemnation of war must be understood.

Thirdly, Kant's account of the machinery required for inaugurating and extending peace is skimpy in the extreme. From one point of view this is natural enough. All constructive political philosophy is necessarily programmatic. Philosophy does not offer practical or detailed solutions to political problems. Its job is to reveal the logical lay-out, the geometry and the contours of the main areas within which political problems arise, so that we can at least agree about the *kinds* of solution that they admit of. But this answer cannot wholly excuse Kant on the present issue, within which problems of principle also arise. Kant's reliance upon mediation and arbitration for the settlement of inter-state

conflicts rests upon a far too easy assumption of the feasibility of legal
*and acceptable* settlements in such cases. Are legal settlements or judgments in this area – or indeed in any area – likely to be respected unless
they are backed by force or the threat of force? We may (most of us)
obey the law most of the time without thinking about its enforceability,
but do any of us do so *all* the time? Again, to come back to international politics, while weaker powers might be expected to accept un-
pleasant judicial settlements – since otherwise still harsher conditions
would be forced upon them by their stronger neighbours – can we
expect stronger powers to bow to the decisions of a physically powerless
arbitrator or tribunal? More generally, whenever conflicting parties
accept a judicial settlement, or whenever, as a result of mediation, they
reach a compromise or strike a bargain, is not the thought of greater
strength, of a power of ultimate enforcement, *somewhere in the background* always a most decisive factor in producing the result?

This last point suggests, however, that our present criticism has been
carried too far. For Kant, with his grimly realistic view of human life,
would have been the last man to suggest that it could ever be entirely
freed from rivalries, claims and counter-claims, alliances of powerful
interests, party and partisan pressures, and, in consequence, all manner
of particular misfortunes and injustices. His case, however, is against
one intolerable form of misfortune and injustice – war; and more
expressly against the claim that war can be regarded as a lawful
method of settling disputes between states. In this connection there are
two things that we must bear in mind. First, international relations, in
Kant's day, were at once much less developed and also much more
consistently ruthless and bloody than they are today. Less ruthless and
bloody forms of inter-state pressure – economic boycott, for instance, or
the mobilisation of world opinion – were as yet untried; so that war and
the threat of war were the main methods of advancing and defending
state interests. To reject war, or rather to brand it as wholly unjust or
anti-law, was, therefore, to expose the current conception of the international order as intolerable in principle. It involved a new start, a new
dispensation, the beginnings of a lawful relation between states in place
of a war-system dressed up in a few legalistic trappings. And until such
a new beginning was made – until the right to go to war was abjured
and reliance upon arbitration was proclaimed by at least a few like-
minded states – all talk of improving the lot of mankind was so much
wasted breath. Secondly, we must remember that Kant's reliance on
arbitration presupposed a general recognition of the ever-increasing cost

31

and destructiveness of war. True, he thought of these disincentives to war in less horrific terms than we have come to do. But his prescience in picking them out as necessary preconditions of perpetual peace is all the more to his credit. He believed that men would be *forced* to accept a new international order, but forced by Nature – by the natural consequences of ever-intensifying wars – not by the wills and weapons of men.

Fourthly, and more generally, Kant's 'guarantee' of perpetual peace – which is in fact the application of his 'philosophy of history' to his project – certainly calls for much closer scrutiny than we have given to it. To examine it in detail would, however, carry us too far from our topic. I will therefore confine myself to two observations, one in defence of, and one in criticism of, this aspect of Kant's thought. Although there are places where Kant's language suggests an almost naively providential view – as when he writes of 'Nature's secret plan' to secure human progress by means which stand in complete contrast to the austere demands of pure Practical Reason – the real thrust of his thought here is sounder than that of any other philosopher who has based an optimistic philosophy of politics upon an interpretation of mankind's political past. In the first place, Kant does not assume, nor does he claim to demonstrate, that human progress has been consistent or that it will always continue. What he urges is that we have a right to plan and act *as if it could* do so, in order to sustain our effort to ensure that it *will* do so. But further, even if his terminology is at times naive and even a little absurd, his political insight is here remarkably sound. Political action is always in the nature of a two-stroke engine: it requires *both* some recognition of timeless truths – what Kant called Reason's demands – regarding just dealing between man and man, society and society; *and also* a sense of what is 'on' politically and what is not, of what is possible, opportune, worth claiming and worth working for in a given period and place and what is not, of what is a fool's game or a dead-end or just too lethal to touch. Kant's moralistic legalism corresponds to the first stroke of the engine of politics: his weirdly worded but perceptive notion of 'Nature's secret plan' – or how mankind's 'unsocial sociability' can serve to stimulate its rational powers and advance its rational destiny – corresponds to the second stroke. The result is a hypothetical interpretation of human history and destiny which does nothing to flatter mankind, yet provides a framework in which Reason's high demands upon men make sense, without offering them either respite or assurance of success.

Kant has, however, no clear, consistent account of the specific role or roles of Reason within 'Nature's secret plan'. His thought moves between the following positions: first that Practical Reason by itself is impotent in the field of politics, i.e. although setting the goals of rational human endeavour, it must wait for the roundabout workings of Nature's plan to realise them:[26] secondly that to assist in realising Nature's plan, not only are all mankind's inventive skills (deriving from Theoretical Reason) required, but great human steadfastness and wisdom (deriving from Practical Reason) also;[27] and finally that in certain special circumstances (Kant optimistically instances the reception of the French Revolution by generous minds in other countries) the precepts of Practical Reason may act 'like a self-fulfilling prophecy', and display an independent capacity to strengthen their usually feeble hold upon human imagination and conduct.[28] Kant's uncertainty as between these positions reflects deeper difficulties and weaknesses at the heart of his philosophical system. But no one, except a fool or a committed metaphysician, would expect a clear-cut answer to a question so central to all human life and action. There are times when it is right to recognise Reason as impotent; times too when we should recognise it as indispensable; and times when we may rightly look to it for our salvation.

This brings us to the merits of Kant's project for perpetual peace. They rest on a number of insights which were, when Kant first struggled to find expression for them, far in advance of their time; indeed no later philosophical thinker seems to have attempted to see them again as the unity which they certainly formed in the philosophy of Kant's old age. It is astonishing how pertinent and how persuasive these insights have become in the light of international developments in our century. This is not a proof of their correctness; but at least it makes them an initially helpful starting-point for reflection on the international system. First we have the insight that while peace-intended-to-be-perpetual is a recently recognised political task, yet logically it has always been required by the idea of mankind as a single moral community, and as such is an imperative for all men and more directly for all governments now, beginning now and for any conceivable future. In this respect we might say Kant has paid the Stoic-Christian ideal of the unity of mankind the supreme compliment of taking its political consequences seriously. Thereupon we have the further insights that peace thus conceived as the quest of justice between men through justice between states is something that still has to be inaugurated; that

33

all known international systems have therefore essentially been war-systems and that all defences of them, even by high-minded international lawyers, have been in effect defences of war; that, thus understood, peace between states is as much a demand of Reason, as is the demand that men shall form states and support state-governments for the enforcement of justice (or protection of basic rights); that the kind of accord that can rationally be expected to work *between* states must, however, rest on entirely different principles from those that ensure (in some degree) justice and security *within* states (so that the idea of a global empire or super-state or international police force provides no solution of the second great problem of politics); that the impossibility of achieving a permanently secure international system provides no objection to its moral and rational compulsoriness – on the contrary the permanent possibility of its failure provides an essential motive for conscientiously working to maintain it; that while the requirements of practical (moral) reason impose and define the task of peace between nations, they are manifestly not sufficient to achieve it; and that aid for this task is to be found, not in considerations of self-interest or utility, but in a general recognition of mankind's chronic condition of 'unsocial sociability' and of the surprising advantages that can be gained by exploiting those ambiguities of human nature which Kant ascribes – perhaps naively, perhaps playfully – to 'Nature's secret plan'. Put more concretely, this last insight amounts to the fact that, given a plurality of sovereign states and given human nature as we know it, voluntary agreement between *all* states to abjure war and replace it by various forms of arbitration or bargaining can be expected only when war has become intolerable and indeed unthinkable – not only morally and economically, but, as we would now add, biologically as well.

Cementing all these insights, we have that dominant tendency of Kant's later philosophy – his persistent urge to explore any area of human experience in which a rationally acceptable form of teleology can be disclosed, and the chasm which he had set between Natural Necessity and Rational Freedom can, in an appropriate sense, be bridged. Although this tendency is not as explicit in *Perpetual Peace* as it is, for instance, in the last book Kant published, *The Conflict of the Faculties*, yet its influence on the former work is unmistakable. Through all the oddities, pedantries, jumpinesses and seeming discontinuities of *Perpetual Peace*, Kant is persistently concerned with the relation between the rational conscience of the free-thinking individual and the tragically blind and wayward, the often hideously misdirected, history of the race to which the individual belongs, not only physically and culturally but in respect of his highest capacities and calling. In this way he was able to present the task of perpetual peace-*making* as, like all the other major tasks of mankind, essentially a matter of man's remaking of himself – of his means of subsistence, his habitat, his institutions, his moral and scientific standards, all considered as special cases of the truth that the proper business of mankind is man. And in this way it can be claimed for Kant, who according to Heine's gibe never *had* a life, that he found himself in his later thought nearer to the heart of human life than most of those who have prated and preached about how to get there.

As against this high claim it might be objected that Kant's actual project for perpetual peace is not as original or unique as I have suggested, and that in particular – despite profound differences in respect of moral foundations – it is surprisingly like that put forward, of course quite independently, by Bentham. Both thinkers insist that improvements in international relations cannot be made or be maintained by force, but must rely on the development of a civilised public opinion. And both combine this position with a strenuous emphasis upon the necessity of force to institute a legal order within particular states. What then, apart from their philosophical predilections, is the real difference between them? Are they not both essentially liberals – essentially over-optimistic liberals – in their attitudes to international affairs? My answer is that while they were both serious lovers of liberty, the seriousness of Kant was of an altogether deeper, more searching kind. Bentham's great achievement, it has been well said, was to make morality business-like – in the sense of leading to political, legal and economic reform. But in the international field Bentham made the mistake of thinking that reform could be left to 'business' in the sense of freely operating international trade. Kant's position was quite different: it was liberalism, not in its early euphoric advance, but already prematurely wise – cautious, contrite, yet completely resolute, ready to hold out till the end of the day, and convinced that in international affairs, as perhaps in certain other areas of human contact and conflict, peace-making must be left to the imperfect experience and always doubtful rationality of the parties involved, because any attempt to enforce peace, conceived as a legal order between independent states, can mean only a renewal of war. Thus, whereas for Bentham the future of international relations looked like plain sailing, to Kant it suggested the toughest of voyages – inescapable, imperative, yet with some hope of safety – across a literally endless sea.

Finally, a word about the philosophical framework within which, despite his efforts at popularisation, Kant inevitably developed his project for perpetual peace. He sought to confine the remarkable insights which we have been discussing under a single rubric – the commands or requirements of Reason (spelt with a very big R). Reason seemed to him, as to many lesser thinkers of the Enlightenment, to be a magic key, capable not only of unlocking all the secrets of the physical world, but of commanding the rational agreement (though not the reliable compliance and allegiance) of ali who heard its call. Kant's conception of Reason, as I have indicated, was an unusually imaginative, flexible and prophetic one – a much more promising candidate for the definition of mankind's 'species being' than that to be suggested some decades later by the young Karl Marx. But, considered as a political watchword, 'Reason' has long since lost its magic; indeed in the vocabulary of modern political science it is little more than an archaism covering a number of branches of technological know-how. But whatever better watchword men may find to replace it we may be sure that it must embody most of the insights that lie behind Kant's doctrine of peace-intended-to-be-perpetual. In particular it must express something very close to Kant's generously felt hopes for the future of mankind, along with his responsible recognition of the fragile, fractious and fallible stuff we humans are made of.

# 3

## CLAUSEWITZ ON THE NATURE OF WAR

To most of us, I suspect, Clausewitz is a somewhat cloudy, mysterious and faceless figure, composed too much of anomalies for definite realisation or understanding. He was a general and a philosopher, reputedly an admirer of Kant and an objective analyst, if not an apologist, of war. If, as has been said, the idea of a literate general defeats the Anglo-Saxon imagination, what can we hope to make of the Prussian officer who was to become the world's first – and, as it may turn out, also its last – philosopher of war? The easiest solution would be to turn him into something definitely repellant – the logician of force, the justifier of bloodshed, or, in Liddell Hart's phrase, 'the Mahdi of mass and of mutual massacre'. And indeed, with a slight change in the balance of historical forces and hence in national mythologies since his death, he might well have become a name of terror, like Bonaparte to nineteenth-century English children. But in fact, what kind of man was Carl von Clausewitz?

The face that looks out from his portraits takes us by surprise. It suggests a poet rather than a philosopher and *a fortiori* than a general. We see a man of medium height and slight build, with red-brown hair, finely formed features and a smile of unusual tenderness. And his letters indicate moral and intellectual attitudes that match his appearance. Apart from his professional and patriotic ardour – he was always an enthusiastic supporter and deviser of military and political reforms – they reveal a man of wide general culture, with a notable capacity for forming deep personal attachments, and a vein of melancholy which turned, in his later years, into almost pathological disappointment with his own achievements. His letters to his wife, in particular, express feelings that go far beyond the elegant protestations of the age. One of them describes, with moving simplicity, his feelings on hearing of the death of Scharnhorst; another, written many years later, speaks of the sadness that he has always experienced on returning

37

to Potsdam where his father had taken him, at the age of twelve, to be enlisted in the Prussian army. His wife's descriptions of him are no less revealing. She was his elder by a year, and a woman of outstanding spirit, devotion and literary and artistic culture. Her family, von Brühle, belonged to the highest Prussian aristocracy, and it took her five years to beat down their objections to her marrying Clausewitz. In her letter to him and in her memoirs she writes of her husband with uninhibited admiration for his moral and intellectual gifts and with a tender concern for his strange personal fragility.

From these introductory impressions let us turn to the salient facts of Clausewitz's life. He was born in Burg, Mechlenburg, in 1780, the third son of a very middle middle-class Prussian family. In 1792 he was enlisted Gefreikorporal in the Prussian infantry, in which his two elder brothers had preceded him; and within two years he had seen military action. Of Clausewitz's years as Gefreikorporal and ensign we know little, except that he was a voracious reader and liked to spend his furloughs on a farm in the Rhineland. It is important, however, to remember that during these early years his lack of noble birth made promotion to the officer corps a very doubtful prospect. Even after he was commissioned, adjustment to the brutal and snobbish military establishment cannot have been easy for the middle-class boy. In 1801, however, he won a place as an officer cadet in the new Berlin War School; and here his great abilities were recognised by Scharnhorst, then director of the school, a man of even humbler origins than Clausewitz, who had nevertheless come to be recognised as the outstanding German soldier of his age. Until his death in 1813, Scharnhorst constantly befriended, encouraged and assisted the younger, more diffident, vulnerable and scholarly man. It was thanks to his influence that Clausewitz was appointed adjutant to Prince August of Prussia, with whom he took part in the Auerstadt and Jena campaigns, in the latter of which he and his prince were captured by the French. Released in 1808, Clausewitz returned to work with Scharnhorst in the Prussian Ministry of War, and soon became a leading member of a small circle of ardent military – and therefore, if willy-nilly, of political – reformers within the officer corps. At the same time he was chosen, because of his literary gifts, to supervise the military education of the Crown Prince; and having now attained the rank of major he was at last able to marry the Countess von Brühle.

Nevertheless, during these seemingly happy years, Clausewitz became increasingly restless, from a mixture of patriotic and professional motives, over the politically degraded position of Prussia, now truncated in its territory and continuously occupied by Napoleon's troops since the Treaty of Tilsit. Early in 1812 Prussia was forced into a defensive alliance with France – actually and evidently aimed against Russia; and this event led Clausewitz to take the most important decision of his life. Encouraged by Scharnhorst and Gneisenau he obtained, in accordance with a common enough custom at the time, his sovereign's release from the Prussian service, and travelled east to join the Russian forces in which several German officers were already serving. Although handicapped by his ignorance of the Russian language, Clausewitz performed some notable services to the Russian cause, as a military adviser and as the chief negotiator of the celebrated Convention of Tauroggen, whereby in January 1813 the Prussian General Yorck proclaimed the release of all his forces from the French alliance. Clausewitz also took part, in the role of staff officer, in the battles of Witebsk, Smolensk and Borodino; and later, when attached to Wittgenstein's army of the north, he followed and saw at close quarters the retreat and disintegration of the Napoleonic Grand Army.

All this gave him an unusually well-balanced insight into the greatest and most terrible military event of his age, and opened his eyes to the possibility of entirely new forms of warfare. But the cost was heavy. His health was permanently impaired; he emerged from the campaign afflicted by some form of rheumatic or arthritic illness which forced him to rely increasingly on opium, and with his face cruelly disfigured by frostbite. Mentally also he was affected by what he saw of the French retreat. He felt, as he remarks in his book on the 1812 campaign, as if he could never again be free from the hideous impressions of the spectacle. But then, with his usual objectivity, he adds that the rate of casualties in the Russian army of the north was almost as high as on the French side. From this point onwards, deep depression and discontent with his career became almost obsessive themes in his letters. And, if he had hoped for a hero's welcome on his return to Prussia, he was to be sharply disappointed. For over ten years he was treated with persistent dislike and distrust by the government of King Frederick William III. Alone among the officers who had joined the Russian service in 1812, he was persistently refused readmission to the Prussian army during the 1813–14 campaigns, despite the pleas of Gneisenau and other friends. His plans for a popular militia (*Landsturm*) to support the regular army against the French were dismissed as a recipe for revolution. It was not until 1815 that he was allowed to return to the

Prussian army as chief of staff of Thielmann's corps in the Waterloo campaign.

After the war he had an enjoyable year as Chief of Staff to Gneisenau with the German Rhine Army. Here he began to sketch his book *On War*. But in 1818 he was recalled to Berlin, to act as administrative director of the new War School, a post which proved to be half sinecure, half insult. Clausewitz hoped to be able to reform the syllabus and spirit of the school's teaching, but was persistently over-ridden by a conservative-minded board with which all real power of decision lay. Certainly the post gave him ample time to write the books that he had long been planning – not only *On War* but a number of histories of eighteenth- and early nineteenth-century campaigns. But the inactivity which the post imposed upon him, and the realisation that he would now never obtain an important military command, irked him painfully. Only in the crisis of 1830 was he recalled to active service, and to his delight was again appointed Chief of Staff to Gneisenau on the Eastern Front. But here further disappointment awaited him. He soon recognised that he was physically unfit for his task, and, perhaps an even more cruel blow, that his old comrade was no longer the heroic figure whom he had once so ardently admired. There were disagreements and signs of unease between the two men, although Gneisenau constantly leaned on Clausewitz's advice. Fate struck suddenly in the form of the cholera epidemic of 1831, which carried off Gneisenau and Hegel amongst countless others. Clausewitz succumbed to it so quickly that some have suggested that the cause of his death was in fact an aneurism or some form of nervous seizure. He was only fifty-one years of age.

The personality and character which we glimpse through this strangely varied career, as well as through his writings, letters and the reports of his contemporaries, must remain in some ways an obscure one; but its basic pattern is by no means cloudy, faceless or unintelligible. That he should have possessed the cardinal soldierly virtues – courage, endurance, good-heartedness and loyalty to his commanders – and yet have lacked the infectious self-assurance that is required of a great commander at any level, need not surprise us: able military men are not more necessarily all of a piece than men in other walks of life. Nor is it unintelligible that a man who, in social relations, showed a certain diffidence and a need of others, older and more confident than himself, to push him forward, should at the same time have been capable of taking bold, difficult, lonely decisions, and could, when once caught up in military debate, produce questions, criticisms and arguments of an outstanding clarity and persuasiveness. Nor is it strange that these intellectual gifts should have existed side by side with other more morally ambiguous qualities that can greatly aid a military leader: constant ambition to shine in the military field, a prickly sense of personal honour, and a dangerous capacity to idealise any cause – whether army, country or alliance – to which he had committed himself. And these qualities in turn lead on to others that reveal the more fragile side of his nature: brief spells of almost frenzied enthusiasm and audacity, punctuated by moods of bitter exasperation and intolerance, and – especially in his later years and after the collapse of his health – by longer spells of acute depression.

It would, however, be a mistake to regard Clausewitz as a misfit: an intellectual, and indeed a 'sensitive', compelled to see his talents neglected or despised in the barrack-room atmosphere of the Prussian state. He was every inch a man of his age, in which a surprising number of military officers proved themselves at least the equals, in intellectual culture, of their civilian peers. And it is difficult to believe that the hardship, short-comings and disappointments of his career did not serve him well when he set about systematising his ideas on the general conduct of war. Certainly in this task – which to the eye of history was his life's work – he showed a dedication to the maxim 'Know thy trade' that is comparable to that which the greatest of philosophers have accorded to 'Know thyself' or 'Know the limits of thy knowledge'. If he had not achieved greatness in war, he was to bring the greatness of war under his intellectual command. He would make clear, for himself and for minds of his own calibre, what it was about, what it could and could not achieve, how it worked in so far as it worked, and how it was likely to develop – in so far as such prediction was possible. And from this point of view the disappointments of his career, and his failure to exercise high command mattered not at all. For he had observed at close quarters, with admiration qualified at once by a noble envy and a cool detachment, so many great commanders in so many crucial situations; and from his vantage-point, at their elbows, he had been able to distinguish and balance in thought – and was later able to delineate in words – problems, issues and principles which a Scharnhorst or a Kutuzov, or for that matter a Napoleon, could never have articulated with such clarity and power. What brought him to this task? Here is his own brief account of how *On War* came to be written:

These materials have been amassed without any preconceived plan. My aim was at first, without regard to system and strict connection, to put down the results of my reflections upon the most important points in quite brief, precise, compact propositions. I thought that concise, striking chapters would attract the attention of the intelligent as much by what was evidently to be developed from them as by what they contained in themselves. I had, therefore, before me in idea readers already acquainted with the subject. But my nature, which always impels me to development and systematising, at last worked its way out in this instance also...The more I advanced with the work, and the more I yielded to the spirit of investigation, so much the more I was led to system; and thus, then, chapter after chapter has been inserted...I now aim to go through the whole once again, and to establish by further explanation many of the earlier theses; for my ambition has been to write a book which would not be forgotten within two or three years, and which anyone interested in this subject would certainly take up more than once.[1]

It seems to me that whether these words were prefixed to a treatise on war or a treatise on peace – or on law or on rhetoric or on logic or mathematics or economics or engineering or navigation – no one with the slightest acquaintance with philosophy could fail to suspect that their author was a man of marked philosophical ability. They display the comprehensive view, the poise, the slightly ironic self-awareness, the modesty and the assurance that are necessary to any work of value in that field. They are the words of a man who knows very well what he is about, and yet also how little – and at best how one-sidedly – he can convey that knowledge. Above all they suggest a man who realises to what an extent any thinker is in the hands of his work, that *his* best work is when *it* takes over, and that his main duty is to ensure that this happens as often as possible. Which suggests a genuine, if not a great, philosopher.

What, then, were Clausewitz's main contributions to philosophy? They were naturally of a limited kind; but they would have been much appreciated by Aristotle, and, oddly enough, by some of the ablest philosophers of our century. One could say, in the current jargon, that they were centred on the *idea* of *practice* and its implications for social science in general. But first let us appreciate, what today might seem commonplace but at his time was a notable achievement, his placing of the study of war among other intellectual inquiries. He rejects all attempts to assimilate war either to the mechanical arts, e.g. engineering, which are based on objective laws that have been found to hold for all physical systems, or to the fine arts for which, in his opinion, no firm principles can ever be established, despite general agreement about the masterpieces they produce. As against these views he insists that war belongs

to the province of social life. It is a conflict of great interests, which is settled by bloodshed, and only in that is it different from others. It would be better, instead of comparing it with any Art, to liken it to business competition, which is also a conflict of human interests and activities; and it is still more like state policy, which again may be looked upon as a kind of business competition on a grand scale. . .The essential difference consists in this, that War is not an activity of the will exerted upon inanimate matter like the mechanical arts, or upon a living but passive and yielding subject, like the human mind and the human feelings as in the case of the fine Arts, but against a living and re-acting force.[2]

In other words, the conflicting interests, aims, means and moves in which war consists continually affect each other reciprocally, and most importantly through the continual attempts of either side to conceal its intentions, to deceive, surprise and out-manoeuvre its opponent, and at the crucial point to outmatch him in strength. And taking these facts in conjunction with the inevitable shortage and imperfection of true information in war, Clausewitz concludes – against certain theorists of his age and certain technically sophisticated although practically trivial war-theorising of our age – that the ideal of a logically complete or sufficient 'answer' to any problem in warfare is a sheer delusion.

But this does not mean that there can be no theory, and no theory-based rules, of warfare. This, Clausewitz maintains, only follows if we adhere to an excessively – indeed pedantically – narrow idea of what theory is and does. There are certain aspects of the world that admit of a highly systematic theoretical understanding such as is afforded by physics. But there are other aspects of the world, and in particular of human action, that neither admit of nor require such systematic treatment, and yet evidently stand in need of theory of some kind if such understanding as we have of them is to be safeguarded and developed. Theory exists and operates, Clausewitz maintains, wherever a set of general rules or maxims manifestly aids judgement or decision, even if it lacks that logical sufficiency for the solution of problems which all pure science aspires to.[3] This brings us to two of Clausewitz's most impressive philosophical achievements: his accounts of the logical character or status of the principles of war, and of the stance or style of thought which the realities of war demand of commanders at any level. On both these issues what he has to say has important implications for human life far beyond the military field.

Clausewitz discusses a number of 'principles of war', but it is notable that he nowhere tries to deduce these principles from any single source or to establish relations of logical priority and subsequence between them. Moreover in this connection he displays a curious and at first sight irritating habit. He will lay down some principle which immediately commends itself to common sense, that of constancy in one's objective, or of concentration or economy or security in the use of forces, for example; but he thereupon proceeds to show how some other principle of war commonly interferes with it, to modify or even cancel its authority in certain situations. His purpose in proceeding thus, however, is of the first importance. It is to show that, besides never being *sufficient* to decide what must be done in any war-situation, no principle of war is ever *necessary* to a right military decision, in the sense that it cannot be contravened. But the principles of war *are* necessary in a subjective or educational sense, in that they severally call attention to situations, developments, chances, dangers, which continually recur in war, and are liable to be of crucial importance in deciding the issue between success and disaster. No competent commander ever *forgets* an established military principle, but every competent commander must be prepared to *override* even the most seemingly central of military principles, in certain emergencies.

Military principles have to be simple, Clausewitz continues, in the sense of suggesting the advisability or inadvisability of certain possible moves for certain quite familiar reasons; for nothing that is inherently complex, nothing that is conditional upon the co-operation of a wide variety of factors, is ever worth attempting in war.[4] At the same time, however, military principles have to be highly adaptable, so that they can assist the commander to take account of any number of changes and developments which may turn out to be significant. This explains why the logical character, and in particular the relationship, of the principles of war are at first sight so curiously loose. Another important fact follows from the need of adaptability: a commander must carry his principles 'live' in his mind, for their method of application on a given occasion may be such as could not possibly have been foreseen.

In almost all other arts and occupations the agent can make use of truths which he has learnt, but in whose spirit he no longer lives, e.g. truths extracted from dusty books. Even truths which he uses daily may remain quite external to himself. . .he applies them as if by mechanical dexterity. But it is never so in war. The fact that he is concerned with *re*-action, and the ever-changeful face of things, makes it necessary for a commander to carry in himself the whole living apparatus of his knowledge, so that

44

anywhere and at any pulse-beat he may be capable of giving the right decision from himself. Knowledge must, by this complete assimilation with his own need and life, be converted into power. This is the reason why everything seems so easy with men distinguished in war, and why everything in it is commonly ascribed to natural talent. . .in contradistinction from what is learnt by prolonged observation and study.[5]

This point is pressed home in a number of passages, as when Clausewitz tells us that in war theoretical truths are most effective when they pass 'from the objective form of knowledge to the subjective one of skill in action',[6] or that 'in war the actor should obey truths of theory rather because his mind is imbued with them than because he regards them as absolute inflexible laws';[7] or that theory should 'guide the future commander in his own self-education',[8] and that its truths exist 'to offer themselves for use as required, and that it must always be left for judgment to decide whether they are suitable or not'.[9] This emphasis upon the subjectivity of military assessments and judgments may seem strange and suspicious to minds brought up to trust only to objective, i.e. publicly establishable, truths. But in fact the subjectivity upon which Clausewitz insists is less a subjectivity of judgment than of responsibility for consequent action. For one thing, a commander's subjective judgments, in Clausewitz's view, are bound to be guided and checked by the educative and suggestive power of the principles of war with which he is imbued. And equally we must remember that, for the practice of war, correctness of judgement is valueless except in relation to the efficacy of the action that it evokes. In any military operation one man must make the final judgment, because there is only one command that can, by its conviction and confidence, set the appropriate operation in movement or give its motion a new force and direction.

Clausewitz describes this aspect of a commander's action in a most original and suggestive way. He remarks 'how the greatest generals speak of war in the plainest and briefest manner, how the government and management of this ponderous machine, with its hundred thousand limbs, is made no more of on their lips than if they were speaking of their own persons, so that the whole tremendous act of war is personalised into a kind of duel . . .'.[10] And he then adds that 'this facile *coup d'oeil*, this simple art of picturing things, this personification of the whole action of war, is so entirely and completely the right way of conducting war, that in no other but this broad way could anyone attain that *freedom of mind* [my italics] which is indispensable if one is to dominate events and not be overpowered by them.'[11] This seeming simplicity of the knowledge

45

required of any military commander does not imply that anything in war is easy, or that any military operation can be carried through without a good deal of technical knowledge, mastery of routines, etc., by all those involved in it. Nor does it rule out the possibility that a commander in action may not sometimes envisage his problem in highly abstract, mathematical terms. Clausewitz's point is, rather, that the act of unifying and directing all the various capacities and efforts that are necessary to success in any act of war, calls for something much more akin to a man's (and in particular an athlete's) awareness of and control over his own body than to the kinds of knowledge with which philosophers (up to his time) had generally concerned themselves, e.g. the understanding of a mathematical principle or of a fairly complex piece of machinery, or even the mastery of a complex technique. Of course Clausewitz is not claiming that the power to 'picture and personalise' situations is sufficient to ensure success in warfare, only that some degree of it is necessary to all such success, since no one can *command* a military operation unless he unites it by directing it – just as he does his own physical balance, movements and exertions. And again it is obvious that this part of Clausewitz's teaching has implications that go far beyond the military sphere.

It would be interesting to relate this account of military thinking to Clausewitz's discussion of the use of military history, and the critical study of the best documented battles and campaigns, in the training of future commanders – a discussion in which he anticipates R. G. Collingwood's idea of history as the re-enactment of past deeds, while yet taking account of the 'hard' facts of history, which Collingwood, with his idealist predilections, either minimises or ignores.[12] I think, however, that I have said enough to indicate how original and how strong Clausewitz's philosophical capacities were. It has been important to stress this for two reasons. First, because while the German, French and American expositors have shown some respect for his philosophy – often to be sure with only the haziest notion of what it was all in aid of – his best-known British critics, the late Sir Basil Liddell Hart and the late Major-General Fuller have regarded it as either of minor importance or as so much moonshine. Not that these critics of Clausewitz are without excuse for their characteristically Anglo-Saxon attitudes. For – and this is my second reason for emphasising Clausewitz's philosophical competence – when we come to his most celebrated and, for our purposes, his central problem – the relation between what he calls Absolute War and Real War (or War conceived as a Political Instrument) – we will find that he falls into grave philosophical confusions; and the task of cutting our way through these to the geneuine insight which they obscure calls both for sympathy with his difficulties and respect for his normal capacity to express his thoughts simply and clearly. One of the ironies of the situation is that, in dealing with the philosophical issues so far discussed, Clausewitz does very well with his own unprofessional but carefully considered arguments and analyses, which fully merit Marx's comment that 'the fellow has the kind of common sense that comes close to wit'.[13] It is when he leans upon what he takes to be accepted philosophical terms and methods – whether those of the great philosophers of his age or those of the decadent traditional logic which he had the misfortune to inherit – that his touch fails and that he lapses into errors and equivocations.

The difficulties that now face us are not confined, however, to matters of terminology, logic and method. They are also due to the fact that *On War* was left unfinished, or at least imperfectly revised, at Clausewitz's death. We know that his serious reflections and writings towards a comprehensive treatise on 'Grande Guerre' date from 1816, and that by 1827 he had sketched out all eight books of *On War*. The celebrated 'Notice' of 1827 – a kind of interim preface – expresses his intention to revise the whole work on the basis of a much simpler (and to my mind more promising) terminology. But although Clausewitz had made considerable revisions of Books 1–6 by 1830, the only chapter with which he was then satisfied was Book 1 chapter 1. And here, far from simplifying his terminology and principles, he had, if anything, complicated them in his efforts to produce a consistent preliminary statement of the structure of his military thought. Leaving aside the many minor complications which this involves, we are thus faced – as all readers of Clausewitz will always be faced – with the following difficulty. Book 1 chapter 1 of *On War* stands apart from the remaining chapters, in that it offers an extended treatment, and also a radically altered application, of a framework of ideas which Clausewitz had used over many years but had never before tried to articulate and defend in systematic fashion. The question therefore arises: are we to treat this chapter as the *locus classicus* for understanding the logical structure of *On War*? Most commentators point to its later date, evidently careful revision, complex structure and seemingly well-balanced conclusion, and favour it on these grounds. But, on the other side, it could be urged that the cost of smoothing out the sharp antitheses which characterise other relatively unrevised passages of *On War* has been too great; and that the conclusions of the revised opening chapter lack the penetrative power – or the promise of penetration and illumination – which is so strongly conveyed in many (relatively) unrevised passages of *On War*.

I have no wish to engage in this scholarly debate which rests, in my belief, upon two curiously naive assumptions.[14] First that Clausewitz would necessarily have remained satisfied with Book 1 chapter 1 as we now have it after he had tried to revise, in the light of it, a number of related passages in Books 1–4 and 8 in particular. For these revisions would have had to be of a most extensive, indeed transforming kind; and the attempt to make them might well have opened Clausewitz's eyes to certain weaknesses – including the near-banality of the conclusion – of his revised opening chapter. But secondly, the scholarly debate rests on a more general assumption: viz. that the framework of ideas which Clausewitz employed from 1804 onwards in all his more general discussions of war (although with notably different emphases and qualifications) does in fact admit of some one evidently preferable, correct, authoritative and satisfactory interpretation. Yet the more we examine that framework, within which Clausewitz struggled to systematise and defend his central insights over so many years, and the more seriously we ask ourselves what attracted him to it and where he could have found it, the less likely we are to regard it as sacrosanct, or as indispensable for the appreciation of the different and sometimes conflicting strands in his thought. The conceptual framework in question has, to my knowledge, never been adequately unpacked, scrutinised, and reconstructed for comparative purposes; it has never been submitted to systematic logical criticism; and the question of its main philosophical source or inspiration has never even been raised.

I want to show, in the pages which now follow, that Clausewitz's conceptual framework, as articulated in Book 1 chapter 1, is fatally flawed; and that until its flaws are understood, and until it is replaced by something much simpler and logically sounder, the unity of his thought must remain blurred – even its most brilliant insights have to be seized as if through a fog of mystification and distortion. This, I am convinced, has been the experience of many of the most intelligent and sincere readers of *On War*. They have struggled to grasp, accept and apply a framework of ideas, centred on the contrast between Absolute War and Real War, but have failed to recognise that – as with other great but obscure philosophers – Clausewitz's special framework of ideas may well have helped him to get an initial purchase upon his problems, but that thereafter it may have exercised a fatally restrictive and distorting influence upon his handling of them. In saying this I am not suggesting that Clausewitz must therefore remain an impenetrably obscure thinker, the reserve of a few learned and logically skilled specialists, who alone can separate out what is best in him from what is confused and fallacious. On the contrary, it would be truer to say that I want to rescue Clausewitz from the Clausewitzian specialists. For, excellent and indispensable work though they have done in the way of detailed elucidation, it has not occurred to them to ask whether his conceptual system is intelligible *per se* or when compared with other conceptual systems found in the social sciences. They have proceeded – and this is often the way with dedicated expositors of obscure philosophers – as if they were unfolding an exceptional corner of the intellectual universe, which admits of no useful comparison with other familiar regions, but must be understood – followed or pieced together – in its own peculiar terms. But without the possibility of comparison, and hence of criticism, there can be no genuine understanding. And it seems to me intolerable that so much in Clausewitz should have remained, for most of his readers, veiled in a semi-intelligibility which a little criticism and reconstruction could easily have dispersed; the more so since his weaknesses and failures are mainly due to his unhappy philosophical, and more specifically his logical, inheritance.

As everyone knows who has read even cursorily in *On War*, its central problem lies somewhere between two groups of statements, which I shall here exemplify from Book 1 chapter 1. Statements 1–5 come from the opening sections of this chapter, statements 6–10 from its concluding sections. Statements 1 and 10 give us, respectively, Clausewitz's initial ('one level') and his final ('three-level') definitions of war.

(1) 'War is an act of violence intended to compel our opponent to fulfil our will.' (2) '[In its "element" or essence] war is nothing but an extended duel, e.g. between two wrestlers, in which each tries to throw his adversary and thus render him incapable of further resistance.' (3) 'As the use of physical violence by no means excludes the use of intelligence, it comes about that whoever uses force unsparingly, . . . finds that he has the advantage over him who uses it with less vigour.' (4) 'Hence, as each side in war tries to dominate the other, there arises a reciprocal action which must escalate to an extreme.' And for this reason (5) 'The disarming or destruction of the enemy. . .or the threat of this. . .must always be the aim in warfare.' Thus Clausewitz, introducing his idea of Absolute War.

Moving on to the second group of statements we have: (6) 'War is a political act. . .also an effective political instrument, a continuation of political commerce and a carrying out of this by other means.' (7) 'Under no circumstances is war to be considered as an independent thing. . . Policy is interwoven with the whole action of war and must exercise a continuous influence upon it. . .' (8) 'Wars must differ in character according to the motives and circumstances from which they proceed.' (9) 'The first and greatest and most decisive act of the statesman or general is to understand the kind of war in which he is engaging, and not to take it for something else, or to wish it was something else which, in the nature of the case, it cannot possibly be.' (10) 'War. . .is a wonderful trinity, composed of the original violence of its elements, of the play of probabilities and chance which make it a free activity of the soul, and of its subordinate nature as a political instrument, in which respect it belongs to the province of Reason. . .' Thus Clausewitz, introducing his idea of Real War, or of War conceived as a Political Instrument.

All commentators are agreed that Clausewitz's greatest difficulty was to explain the relationship between these two 'ideas of war'; and almost all commentators have assumed that his logical apparatus was adequate to the task of showing whether our two groups of statements are as contradictory, or at least as contrary, as they appear to be, or whether perhaps they are in some sense complementary, or stand in some relation of subordination one to another. On this score there is evidence of at least four different positions held at different times by Clausewitz, at different stages of the writing of *On War*. The first position, which dates from his essay *Strategy* of 1804, is that the only proper military aim being the destruction (or disablement) of the enemy (as in statements 3–5 above) any political considerations which would act as a brake on this must by definition hinder effective military action.[15] The second position is more moderate. Every commander must take into account *both* the essential military aim – destruction or disablement of the enemy – *and* the political aims and conditions which lie behind and indeed motivate any actual war. Somehow – and Clausewitz can produce no formula to explain exactly how – the commander must endeavour to reconcile these two aims wherever they conflict. The third position is that in every such conflict primacy must be given to political considerations. Military exigencies may sometimes briefly obscure this truth: but war could not be understood at all – could not, in strictness, function at all – except under political direction and control.[16] The fourth position carries this last line of thought much further. The conflict between military and political aims, as so far granted, is more apparent than real. Behind every war, of whatever degree of intensity and destructiveness, lie political conditions and decisions which match with *and explain* that degree of intensity and destructiveness. Despite appearances, no war is any more or any less politically directed than any other. If policy is petty, nicely calculated or hesitant, so will be the military moves which it requires. On the other hand 'if policy is grand and powerful, so always will be the war, which may thus approach its *absolute form*'.[17]

We could condense and generalise these different positions by asking: Is the logical picture of war as an essentially self-divided activity, with political claims and conditions pulling in one direction and purely military demands in another, to be preferred to that of war as an essentially unified activity – under the aegis of state policy – a condition which serves to unify, for the purposes of theory, wars of apparently the most diverse characters and intensities? But rather than try to decide between these two pictures of war, I want now to challenge the assumptions that are common to both pictures. And for this purpose, although Clausewitz's idea of War as a Political Instrument is usually regarded as the apogee of his military thought, it is on his idea of Absolute War that we must focus our attention. For, while his account of War as a Political Instrument may be criticised in certain particulars, there is no problem about the meaning of the terms involved. The position is far otherwise with the idea of Absolute War. This is a term of art, whose place in his thought Clausewitz nowhere explains as fully as its importance requires. I shall therefore try now to show how Clausewitz hit on the idea of Absolute War and came to regard it as the principal key to all understanding of war, and how, later, he tried to present it as a necessary consequence of his (first) definition of war and also of what we mean or have in mind whenever we use the general term 'war' in abstract or theoretical reasoning. In this way we can get a sufficiently clear grasp of what Clausewitz's conceptual system or framework amounts to, and can also see why it should not be accepted as the necessary basis of his central teachings on war.

Clausewitz's conceptual system rests on the assumption that our two groups of statements, 1–5 and 6–10 (pp. 49 and 50 above), do not simply describe and oppose two great forces or interests which find expression in all wars: these forces or interests – and their ostensible opposition – are, it is assumed, *necessarily imposed upon our thought* the moment we set ourselves to think clearly and systematically about war's general nature. We then see that statements 1–5 show us the inner logic of the operation of war, while statements 6–10 reveal its essential social function. What, then, led Clausewitz to believe that war's inner logic is contained in his idea of Absolute War?

We *know* nothing of the origin of this idea in Clausewitz's thought. But I believe that we can conjecture with reasonable confidence one fact of importance in this connection. There is good evidence that Clausewitz was in some way much influenced by Kant, although just how remains uncertain.[18] But there are strong reasons for thinking that it was in respect of his methodology, since an essential feature of his conceptual framework closely follows a methodological principle with which all Kant's readers are familiar. Stripped of technicalities it comes to this. In establishing any major division within human interests, for instance between formal and empirical knowledge or between the rational and the animal (or mechanical) elements in human conduct, Kant thinks that the principle of the division should be stated in the sharpest, most extreme possible form – as if, for instance, there could be (what in fact there is not) conduct that is wholly rational or knowledge that is wholly without sensuous content. Once our principle of division (which with Kant is almost invariably dichotomous) has been established in this extreme, unmistakable form, then we can safely consider any factors which may seem to modify it in particular cases. Clausewitz uses this methodological principle at every stage of his thought up to his final revision of Book 1 chapter 1 in order to distinguish war from other forms of organised social action; and the result is his idea of Absolute War. Given that war is distinguished from other forms of social action by the ways in which it employs violence, then its use of violence must initially be grasped in its extreme form, in which there is not a trace of an overlap with processes of bargaining, of persuasion, or of non-military pressure of any kind.[19] And this means the use of violence for complete victory at whatever cost, i.e. the complete destruction or disablement of the enemy's forces. Now we know that Clausewitz attended Kiese-wetter's lectures on Kant, while at the Berlin War School in 1803; and the idea of Absolute War appears, in effect if not in name, in an essay on Strategy which he wrote in the following year. It therefore seems to me highly probable that this idea is Kantian in origin or at least in inspiration: which is not of course to claim that Clausewitz had any detailed or even first-hand knowledge of Kant's writings, or any great insight into his philosophy.

As thus far explained, the idea of Absolute War has no substantial status. Indeed it seems clear that in certain fields a distinction framed in accordance with Kant's principle might prove to be sadly misleading. (Suppose we were to proceed in political studies on the principle that every party or other grouping must be defined in terms of its most extreme members or manifestations). But, from the outset, Clausewitz seems to have felt that, in the idea of Absolute War, he had hit upon something more than a methodological principle – that he now possessed a talisman or guide towards what, with deliberate vagueness, I will call 'the most important fact about war'. And this belief was soon strengthened by two considerations, which I can mention only briefly here. First, it seemed to him that Napoleon owed his success to the fact that he planned his campaigns and battles in ways that approximated closely to the idea of Absolute War, whereas his opponents planned theirs as if the issue – against Napoleon – were a matter of some minor territorial loss or gain. Napoleon may not have taught the world what war *is*, as a matter of fact or as a general rule; but, in Clausewitz's belief, he had certainly taught the world how wars should be fought, granted that war is a serious business, in which the issues can well be the survival or extinction of nations. Secondly, when Clausewitz came to write papers and chapters on military training, he noticed that traditionally acknowledged principles of tactics and strategy are much more clearly and effectively exemplified in wars that approximate to the Absolute form, than they are in those which he described, at one stage of his thought, as 'half-wars': that is wars whose inner logic is concealed or confused by the interference of political considerations which in no way contribute to the effective pursuance of the war.[20]

These are impressive considerations which go some way towards explaining Clausewitz's belief that the idea of Absolute War either was or at least pointed to 'the most important fact about war'. But it was not until his final revision of Book 1 chapter 1 that he attempted a formal proof of this position. This finally revised chapter consists in a quite unusually compressed and complicated argument, which brings out the connection in Clausewitz's thought of a number of ideas which elsewhere receive entirely separate treatment – viz. the dialectical relation between attack and defence at all stages and levels of warfare, the intimate relation of what he calls 'friction' in war with all the contingencies and uncertainties, and all the political interferences, to which every war is subject. And in this respect, for well-prepared readers, Book 1 chapter 1 performs a useful service. But for our present purpose

– Clausewitz's concern with the general nature of war – what matters in it is the logical structure of its main argument, which turns out to be utterly inadequate and confused, and in places plainly fallacious. It is of the first importance for Clausewitzian studies to show why this is so, not only because this celebrated first chapter has caused so much obfuscation to countless readers, but because, once its failings are exposed, it is relatively easy to see how Clausewitz could have avoided this, had he only amplified certain suggestions which he makes elsewhere in *On War*. If, therefore, in the next few paragraphs, I seem unduly severe with Clausewitz, it is with a view to rescuing and restating his central insight about war in a form that admits of easier acceptance and application.

Two main difficulties face us when reading Book 1 chapter 1. As suggested by our statements 1–10, pp. 49–50 above, it begins with an argument purporting to prove demonstratively the primacy of the idea of Absolute War – roughly that it expresses the most important fact about war, both in practice and for a theoretical understanding of it; and it changes, about a third of the way through, into a complex argument claiming to show that the idea of Absolute War is, taken by itself, a misleading abstraction, whose uses must be kept subordinate to the idea of War as a Political Instrument. It is in the transition from the first to the second stage of the chapter that difficulties arise. In connection with this there is a second ostensibly terminological difficulty – although it turns out to be much more than this. The first argument, aimed at establishing the primacy of Absolute War, consists in the claim that this idea follows from Clausewitz's first (single level) definition of war: Absolute War is presented as a truth by definition, a necessary truth. The second argument, aimed at down-grading the idea of Absolute War, rests on a doctrine about the meaning of abstract terms or ideas in general, irrespective of how if at all they are defined in some particular theory. Both arguments are compressed and inexplicit to a degree; but there can be no doubt about the functions they are intended to fulfil, or about the broad grounds on which their conclusions are based, or about their both being very bad arguments.

In the first, the required conclusion does not follow from Clausewitz's first definition of war (our statement 1) but from a highly specific *instance* of it (our statement 2). Nor would it have advanced his main aim – to show that the idea of Absolute War expresses the most important fact about war – if his conclusion *had* followed from his definition of war. There is no intrinsic reason why the most important fact about any term should be deducible from its definition: in this sense it may quite well be logically adventitious. Thus it can be claimed that the most important fact about the family is that it serves to maintain private property, and that the most important fact about money is that it facilitates credit; but neither of these functions is deducible from the received definition of the family or of money. Consequently this attempt on Clausewitz's part to provide a formal defence of the primacy of Absolute War, must be pronounced a failure.

Let us turn, however, to the argument by which he seeks, in the later sections of the chapter, to disown the primacy which he had so long accorded to the idea of Absolute War. In so far as this argument urges the importance of friction, uncertainty, and the asymmetry in respect of strength which Clausewitz finds between defence and attack in all known forms of warfare, it is pertinent and impressive. It brings forward a number of considerations which, taken together, show how very difficult, if not impossible, it often is to prepare, conduct and fight a battle in accordance with the principle of Absolute War. And this being so, the primacy which Clausewitz attributes to that idea certainly requires further elucidation and proof – or possible disproof. But in fact Clausewitz provides none of these things. Even before he has raised the above pertinent criticisms, he admits that to accept the idea of Absolute War as the inner logic of all fighting is to turn one's back on some of the most obvious facts of military experience and to indulge in a kind of 'logical dreaming'. How is this extraordinary *volte-face* to be explained?

The pivot of his argument here is the claim – familiar to all readers of Berkeley and of Hegel – that all abstract ideas are falsifications of the real simply because they are, by definition, selective. To abstract is to simplify, and to accept simplification is to be misled. But to this the obvious and sufficient retort is that all comparison, all generalisation, all theory, indeed all thought, involves selection and abstraction of some kind. To think is not to embrace – or to be engulfed by – the totality of the real. It is therefore pointless to impugn any particular abstraction simply for being abstract; the pertinent question, in all cases, is whether some particular abstraction is or is not helpful, illuminating, testable, adequate, within the limits of a given problematic area. Does the idea of Absolute War throw light on certain aspects of war, which otherwise are easily neglected? If so, then it is of real – it may even be of supreme – importance, for military theory and practice alike. But Clausewitz, in the pivotal sections 6 to 8 of Book 1 chapter 1, adopts such a polemical attitude towards abstraction in general, that he neglects these obvious truths. He writes as if there can be no bridge between the simplified abstractions of war-theory, with their fixed simple meanings, and the endlessly complex, variable, 'chameleon-like' character of war as revealed in experience and history. 'War in the abstract' or 'war according to our conception of it' becomes for him something that has no counterpart or justification 'outside our heads': it is 'war on paper', a matter of mere 'paper laws', a kind of 'logical dreaming'.[21] This is an extraordinary conclusion from the man who elsewhere in his book had given so persuasive an account of the necessity (for educational purposes) of general principles of war, and of the need to keep them constantly adapted to the requirements of action.

This part of Clausewitz's thought would provide an ideal hunting ground for students of philosophical logic. It offers unusually 'live' and important examples of the kinds of very general (categorical) error of which philosophers constantly accuse each other but seldom exemplify from works of scientific theory: in particular it rests upon a perfect text-book case of the so-called 'name theory of the meaning of general terms'. But rather than pursue its errors further, I prefer here to replace it by a reconstruction based on many other passages from *On War*, of what seem to me to have been the positive, even if unconscious, grounds of Clausewitz's long sustained, even if finally rejected, obsession with the idea of Absolute War. The reconstruction which now follows enables us to appreciate how he could have so long regarded the idea of Absolute War as of supreme importance to war-theory, while yet knowing that it was contradicted by the plainest facts of military experience. It contains five stages.

(1) To fight means to try to inflict physically hurtful or disabling physical changes – most obviously blows, but also twists, falls and all manner of other incapacitations – upon an active opponent. (2) The more intensively we deliver, for instance, our blows, the less tolerable the situation becomes for our opponent; and, if delivered with sufficient intensity at the right places, they will break either his power or his will to fight on. (An extreme case of the former – he is killed; of the latter – he surrenders unconditionally). (3) The prospect or fear of such a result may induce our opponent to stop fighting long before the result itself is reached; but this possibility cannot affect the way – the only logical way – in which we should conduct the fight (or war): viz. by applying from the outset and for as long as necessary all the force that we can command. (4) Everything that has been said so far 'from our side' holds

true equally from our opponent's side: either party, if logical, must therefore fight in the manner and with the means that maximise his chance of winning completely, even if that goes beyond his actual interests, and in the knowledge that his opponent, if logical, will do the same. (5) This is the principle of Absolute War. How its logic can be reconciled with, or subordinated to, the calculating, often compromising logic of statecraft, is Clausewitz's central problem.

The problem thus posed is an unreal or unnecessary one; because it rests on a logical blunder at stage 3. Where we affirmed 'this possibility *cannot* affect the way...' all that we were entitled to affirm was 'this possibility *need* not affect the way...in which we should conduct the fight (or war)'. For it is easy to see that if our opponent is likely to agree to stop fighting, on terms that would be advantageous to us, then logic requires that we at least ask ourselves whether further fighting *à l'outrance* is rational. It might then be seen to be appallingly wasteful; it might actually destroy the chance of an advantageous peace to which a lessening of our military pressure would have led. Admittedly it might turn out that neither of these considerations is sufficient, in a particular case, to justify a lessening of our military pressure upon an opponent. But emphatically they are the kinds of consideration which intelligent governments have often explored and exploited, in order to bring a burdensome war to an advantageous close. And since this is so, we have grounds for a more general doubt about the claim made at stages 3 and 4, that there is only *one* logical way of fighting which is to maximise one's chance of winning, *completely*.

There are a number of passages in *On War* which might be said to build upon, or to give a positive form to, this last criticism. Most obviously in the 'Notice' of 1827 he asserts that there are two radically different kinds of war: one (Absolute War) in which the aim is the complete 'disablement' of the enemy, so that we can impose upon him whatever terms we choose, the other in which the aim is to gain certain advantages (particularly territorial) over the enemy which can later be used as bargaining counters at the peace table. Clausewitz remarks that 'transitions' from one kind of war to the other will always occur, but that, nevertheless, the dominant tendencies of war *for such different ends* will always be apparent. This would suggest that there are two ways or styles of fighting wars, corresponding to the two aims, yet admitting of a transition or slide from one to the other in the course of any actual war. But, as already noticed, Clausewitz did not develop this line of thought in his final revision of Book 1 chapter 1.

Again, throughout Book 1 chapter 2 Clausewitz insists that while there are plainly many different ends or objectives in war, yet the characteristic – the ever-necessary and in the end only sufficient – means in war is the combat, or fight. This is the common or mediating element which explains the possibility of the transition between the two kinds of war described in the 'Nctice'. In the former – which, for convenience, I shall from now on call 'knockout wars' – blows are kept up constantly, and in the main in a single direction, with a view to disabling an enemy at his weakest point. In the latter – which I shall from now on call 'advantage wars' – blows are struck wherever the enemy is vulnerable, with a view to damaging and disadvantaging – and discouraging – him in a general way.[22] The former way of fighting may be rarer and more costly; but its successes, if achieved, are incomparably greater. The latter way of fighting, on the other hand, would appear to admit of much finer adjustments and thus to be a more sensitive tool of state policy (a point to which we shall return later on). At the beginning of a war of advantage each contestant will set his probable gains against their probable and tolerable cost. If, in the event, the latter becomes too high for him, he can cool off or call off the war, and accept his disappointing losses in preference to even more intolerable losses. But Clausewitz ends this part of the argument on a most surprising note. He warns commanders and governments who favour 'advantage wars' in the belief that they are safe from the worst or costliest disasters, that this belief may deceive them. The most finely calculated strategies, based on balancing one's own and one's opponent's risks and advantages, may leave a too clever commander exposed to an unexpected knockout blow from an opponent whose resources or daring he has underestimated – the most terrible calamity that can ever happen to a commander in war. It is this danger – the permanent possibility rather than the calculated probability of a knockout – that, more than anything else, explains Clausewitz's obsession with Absolute War. It must always be at the very forefront of a commander's mind because it represents both the very worst and the very best results with which he can be accredited.[23]

This line of thought, which is echoed in many other passages in *On War* was taken up by the greatest of Clausewitz's expositors and critics, Hans Delbrück, who derived from it his doctrine of two types of strategy, that of overthrow (*Niederwerfungsstrategie*) and that of exhaustion (*Ermattungsstrategie*).[24] In this doctrine the main grounds of the transition from one form of warfare to another are brought out with a clarity which Clausewitz does not achieve. It may be doubted, however, whether Delbrück, any more than Clausewitz, recognised the crucial part which the idea of such transitions must play in the elucidation of the concept of war. Both theorists tend to write from the point of view of a commander accepting an assignment and deciding, at the outset, how he can best carry it through – in effect deciding on the lines and character of the coming battle or campaign. But notoriously, the battle or campaign to come may depend as much, if not more, on his opponent's decision as on his own. Here we come close to a point which, as we shall see in chapter 5, greatly impressed Tolstoy: namely that a succession of *ad hoc* improvised moves by two armies may progressively determine, by restricting, each other's future movements and dispositions, until a battle is rendered inevitable, although in circumstances and perhaps with consequences which neither side can properly be said to have planned or chosen or, in any serious sense, to have accepted. Clausewitz shows some appreciation of this point in some of his historical discussions (especially in his account of the 1812 campaign) and, indirectly, in the many passages in *On War* in which he insists on the importance, for every commander, of *persisting in his assigned objective* against the temptation to veer from it as circumstances, danger or opportunity may suggest. What he does not appreciate, however, is that in the course of a campaign, even the most resolute commander may be forced, on pain of the total destruction of his army, to move from one form (aim and strategy) of war to another. The campaigns of Napoleon, whom Clausewitz holds up as the supreme master of knockout war, offer plenty of examples of such enforced changes. But in order to achieve a fuller appreciation of the point here at issue – the central importance of transition from one form of war, or style of fighting, to another – let me close this part of our discussion with a very simple example.

Consider, in this connection, an ordinary boxing bout. It is quite possible that each boxer will start with a clear and definite plan in mind: he will aim at victory on points or at victory by knockout, and, after a little preliminary manoeuvring, will proceed accordingly. But notoriously, a contestant who begins with one plan in mind may be led by opportunity, or by desperation in the face of unexpected resistance, or by the sheer *crescendo* of the struggle, to change his method of fighting in the course of the bout. The threat of a certain points-defeat may drive him into frantic efforts to score a knockout, or the impossibility of securing a knockout may induce him to fight for a bare victory, or a draw, or even an honourable defeat on points. Thus every act of fighting, and not only war, contains in itself the seeds or the possibility of either type of result; and the nature of the result, quite as much as the question of who will be victor, may remain in doubt until the very end of the contest.

Let me now try to sum up my proposed reconstruction of Clausewitz's conceptual system. Clausewitz discerned an essential self-division – sometimes it seemed to him a contradiction – in the planning and execution of any war. He at first equated this division with a simple conflict between the logic of fighting and the political functions and conditions of war. Later he tried to explain it in a number of ways, and eventually he subordinated the logic of fighting entirely to the idea of War as a Political Instrument. But side by side with this development, which culminates in the conclusion of Book 1 chapter 1, there is another strand in his thought: namely that there are two fundamentally different ways of fighting – one in which every exertion is directed to the knockout blow, the other in which position, strength and resources are exploited to obtain any available advantage. Neither of these ways of fighting is more natural or more logical than the other. Each has its use in international relations; each calls for characteristic military effort, skill and discipline; and each demands firm and informed political decision. The great attraction of this second strand is that it does justice to the facts of military history, including the fact that both kinds of war are subject to political direction and control, although no doubt of somewhat different kinds. At the same time, by emphasising the frequent transitions between the two kinds of war, it enables us to do justice to both the following positions: first that, in historical truth, very few wars come near to the Absolute form, and yet, secondly, that the mere possibility of a war approximating to the Absolute form *is and ought to be the* predominant thought in every commander's mind, since it represents either supreme success or the worst disaster that can possibly befall him.

If now it is objected that Clausewitz never fully developed this last point, my retort is that in a number of passages he comes as close to saying it as makes no difference: that it does reconcile, in the sense of doing equal justice to, the two main pulls (and poles) of his military thought; and that it is a position which accords well with his historical vision of war – of the development of war that he had witnessed and of the wholly incalculable future which he ascribed to it. With a few words on this I will conclude.

The accepted view of Clausewitz's philosophy of war is that its core lies in his conception of war as the continuation of policy by the addition of other means, or, more simply, of war as a political instrument. But this view, although advocated by genuine admirers of Clausewitz, is liable to mislead. It suggests that his real interest, even if it is focussed in many of his chapters on specifically military questions, was of a wider kind: it was in politics, and, more particularly, in the relations, tensions and struggles between different political units. This suggestion makes Clausewitz more respectable: for it is widely felt today that, except when it is studied within the wider horizon of politics and sociology, war is a topic as abhorrent in its content as it is weak in theoretical interest. But the simple and obvious truth is that Clausewitz's main interest was in war: in this his book reflects the man, and the man was the mouthpiece of his age. *On War* is emphatically about war, and was primarily written for military men. War is its subject, and the different qualities, relations and dependencies which Clausewitz attributes to war in the course of his book are connected by a single aim: to make clear what this terrible and tragic aspect of human life is about and how it operates. *On War* as many of its expositors have observed, offers us not an apology for war but something much more like a phenomenology of it: a task that is rendered necessary by the fact that it is as difficult to hold up the idea of war, clearly and completely, before consciousness, as it is to perform the same operation with such equally central and elusive ideas as peace, justice, freedom, happiness and love. By contrast, Clausewitz's remarks on politics are (at any rate in *On War*) curiously abstract and meagre. Indeed they are confined to a single brilliant insight, which none of his expositors seems to have noticed, namely that the state is the representative, or agent, of a given community's general interests, *towards other states*. The apparent circularity of the statement in fact expresses Clausewitz's recognition of the all-important truth that to talk of 'the state' *per se* is always misleading: no state would be a state if it did not exist as one of a plurality of other and (at least potentially) rival states. And this is a thought which, given the established tradition of western political philosophy, could hardly have occurred to a thinker who was not preoccupied, principally, with the nature of war.

But the suggestion that Clausewitz was essentially a political theorist (despite his heavy military disguise) is to be rejected on a second count. It would rob him of his uniqueness and originality. Others before him had recognised the crucial role of war in politics – Machiavelli,

Hobbes, Locke, Montesquieu and Rousseau, to mention only the greatest. But Clausewitz's main interest differed radically from theirs. *On War* grew out of his discontent with certain specifically military doctrines, about how to wage and win wars, not about how to use wars in order to achieve such political ends as national security, strength, liberty or whatever. Admittedly, in his more general discussions of the nature of war, Clausewitz calls our attention to aspects of it which are of the first importance for politics, so that *On War* is a work of considerable educative value for political practitioners and theorists alike. But to this we must add that these educative bonuses are always expressed in the most general terms: the last thing Clausewitz would have claimed to be doing in *On War* was to teach politicians their proper business. So true is this, that a common ground of criticism of Clausewitz, especially among his more sociologically minded readers, is that he takes war so entirely for granted, as a going concern, that he shows no positive interest in the particular kinds of social and political situation that are liable to give rise to or prolong or intensify it; still less does he ask how war might be contained or limited or eventually removed from the human scene. In sum, Clausewitz can be criticized, with some cause although not with real justice, for having provided an enlightening anatomy of war – of its action as a whole and of the possible movements of the separate parts – but without adding anything to our understanding of its physiology – the vital forces that call it out and keep it in operation.

These claims and counter-claims, criticisms and rebuttals, regarding Clausewitz's main interests and intentions compel us to attempt something which it never occurred to him to provide: a general characterisation of what might be called his historical vision of war. First, then, he has no political or sociological theory of the main cause or causes of war. Instead he bases all his general discussions upon the extraordinary variety in the aims, means, intensities and levels of sophistication of the wars which history records. One of the most outstanding passages in *On War* – a brilliant birds-eye sketch of the history of war from classical Greece to the Napoleonic age – opens with the following words: 'The semi-barbarous Tartars, the republics of ancient times, the feudal lords and commercial cities of the Middle Ages, eighteenth-century kings and now the rulers and peoples of the nineteenth century, all carry on war in their own way, carry it on differently, with different means, and for different objects.'[25] From this it follows that every war must be studied within its own particular social context, and likewise that, in so far as we must look for permanent causes, elements or principles of war, these must be kept fluid in our thoughts – just as they are in the minds of all great commanders – and must never be allowed to harden into dogmas. Secondly, as regards the future of war, it simply does not occur to Clausewitz to consider the possibility of war's removal from the human scene. This need not surprise us: he here shared the attitude of his peers – philosophers and politicians as much as military men – with only one serious exception, his philosophical master, Kant. What might surprise us, however, is the vehemence with which, in the opening paragraphs of *On War*, he inveighs against those eighteenth-century theorists who had suggested that war might, with the advance of civilisation, be rendered steadily less brutal and bloody, more and more a highly skilled strategic exercise, in which both sides would learn to accept gains and losses in accordance with the 'rules of the game'. As against this superficially optimistic view, Clausewitz insisted that the more serious the motives, the higher the stakes, the more vital the issues, the greater degree of popular involvement on either side, the bloodier and more destructive the resulting war must be.

It would be a great mistake, however, to infer from this that Clausewitz was a brutal militarist, revelling in violently aggressive war. On the contrary – and this is one aspect of his thought which must stagger militarists and pacifists alike – he saw war not only as permanently rooted in the competitiveness of human groups, but as occasioned and kept in being chiefly by those groups, the relatively weaker, 'the harmless defenders', with whom we all feel an immediate and proper human sympathy. As he wittily put it, in sentences which were greatly to delight Lenin when he came upon them in 1915,

The would-be-conqueror [i.e. as we should say, the aggressor] is always a lover of peace (as Bonaparte always claimed to be), for he would like to enter and occupy our state unopposed. It is in order to prevent him from doing this that we must be willing to engage in war, and be prepared for it. In other words it is the weak, or those who will be thrown on the defensive, who need to be armed, so that they shall not be caught out by a surprise attack.

These sentences do not *prove* that war is a permanent necessity for freedom-loving states; but they go a long way towards explaining why the role of war in history has been far from a merely destructive and retroactive one. They also lend support to Professor Howard's interesting suggestion that Clausewitz might conceivably have found Kant's teaching in *Perpetual Peace* (had he construed it aright) quite compatible with his own objective account of the principles of war as disclosed in military history.[26]

But how did this general acceptance of war as an inescapable part of political life affect Clausewitz's view of the European state-system? Here his views were based on those of his enlightenment teachers and yet were developed into a blend of scepticism and heroism that was entirely his own. While he found no evidence of certain or even probable progress in what he knew of European history, he nevertheless believed that, with the emergence of some dozen or so genuinely independent states, no one of which seemed capable of achieving a permanent military preponderance over all the others, there had come into being in modern Europe a kind of political equilibrium which would not easily be overthrown. So long as the majority of independent states shared a common interest in their independence, attempts to create an effective hegemony or empire in Europe were not likely to succeed: witness the careers of Charles V, Louis XIV and Napoleon. Obviously the alleged equilibrium was based upon, and in Clausewitz's view was sufficient to justify, the persistent use of, or at least readiness for, war. But it would be foolish to expect too much from it. While it held out a reasonable prospect of continuing independence for some, perhaps for most European states, it could not promise the survival of any, still less for every, *particular* European state.[27] On the contrary, Clausewitz saw the history of modern Europe as a continuous competitive struggle, always involving risks, sometimes smaller and tolerable, sometimes agonising and lethal – for great and powerful, and for weak and friendless nations alike. Yet the predominant part played by chance in the game of national survival did not itself distress him. From his early years he had recognised the salient place of chance in war; and the fact that it reappeared in the larger game in which war was the main instrument seemed to him only another call for that kind of courage which (to apply one of his finer phrases) is able to leave something to fortune. On the other hand this view of war and of politics generally matched the pessimistic strain in Clausewitz's nature. As he wrote to his then fiancée, at the age of twenty-seven, 'Even the most sublime creations of [human] society carry within themselves the element of their own destruction.'[28]

Modern European war, then, meant for Clausewitz a continuous struggle in which no successes were permanently assured, and no gains, no matter how carefully consolidated, could be expected to last for long. But this was only one aspect of Clausewitz's stoical scepticism with regard to war. There was also the question of its variations in intensity, as between some of the minor dynastic wars of eighteenth-century Europe and between the battles of the nations of 1812/14 in which Clausewitz had taken part. During his lifetime the number and significance of technical innovations in land-warfare had been slight: (apart from the sheer size of the armies which Napoleon tried to control, the most important development, as Clausewitz was among the first to recognise, was in guerilla warfare). He therefore attributed the vast differences in the intensity of wars to one main cause: the degree of involvement, usually on the ground of national survival, of either or both of the peoples concerned. He was thus led to equate wars which 'approach the Absolute point' with what we might call 'wars of embattled democracy'. But here again, with remarkable wisdom, he refused to be drawn into definite prediction and advice. Two of his sentences on this issue are often quoted, but in truth can never be quoted or pondered too often.

Now whether all wars hereafter in Europe will be carried on with the whole power of the states, and consequently will only take place on account of great interests closely affecting the [mass of the] people, or whether a separation between the interests of the Government from those of the people will again gradually arise, would be a difficult point to settle. . .But everyone will agree with us that bounds, which existed only in an unconsciousness of what is possible, when once thrown down are not easily built up again: and that, at least, whenever great interests are in dispute, mutual hostility will discharge itself in the same manner as it has done in our times.[29]

Scepticism? – certainly. Yet with a note of terrible warning that reaches forward a whole century, and has not yet been fully assimilated. Here, as so often, Clausewitz, writing in terms of a style and a scale of warfare which our century has entirely surpassed, nevertheless succeeds in alerting us to the imponderables in our own situation. He forces us back to the supreme paradox of war which is also one of the main paradoxes of politics. We shall be judged by how far we have prepared ourselves to meet the inherently unpredictable, the persistently unexpected.

# MARX AND ENGELS ON REVOLUTION AND WAR

The influence of Clausewitz upon nineteenth- and twentieth-century military theory falls outside the scope of this study. I will only say that the accuracy with which his spirit has been seized by different military theorists seems to me to provide a useful gauge of their intelligence. Thus the elder von Moltke and General de Gaulle (to judge from *Le fil de l'épée*) understood Clausewitz very well from their very different points of view. By contrast Foch and Ludendorff, although quoting him freely, were apparently incapable of mastering any of his key doctrines or for that matter of following any of his sustained arguments. His main British critics, Sir Basil Liddell Hart and Major-General Fuller, adopted a somewhat insular position. Both confessed to seeing gleams of merit in Clausewitz's writings. But to the former his failure to appreciate the British way in continental warfare was unforgivable, while to the latter his addiction to philosophy was his ruin.

There was, however, one group of thinkers who, from the 1850s until the early 1920s, fully appreciated Clausewitz's contributions not only to military thought but to social thought in general – and who drew out some of their most interesting implications. These were the founding fathers of Marxism: Marx himself, despite his many other heavy intellectual preoccupations, but more particularly Engels and Lenin. The main facts about the reception of Clausewitz's ideas by the founders of Marxism have been carefully presented by the contemporary German historian, Dirk Blasius,[1] who has shown, beyond question, not only how seriously the Marxist leaders studied *On War*, but how close to their own central concerns they recognised Clausewitz's teachings to have been. This is a theme to which I will revert at a number of points in the present chapter.

The Marxist leaders' special interest in Clausewitz was only one expression of a more general facet of their thought: their ever increasing concern, after 1849, with the relevance of war and of military force, military preparation and military threats, to their own revolutionary predictions, plans and projects. In calling attention to certain aspects of this concern I am not – let it be understood at the outset – hoping to reveal some monstrous vein of militarism at the heart of Marxist economic and political doctrine. Nothing could be further from my intentions. I cannot forbear from remarking, however, on the way in which the military interests of Engels in particular have been played down by so many British and (until recently) American expositors of Marxism. How many of Engels' British readers – whether among the faithful or among his opponents – are aware that his published writings in the military field outnumber those on all other subjects, and run to over two thousand pages of close print in the complete German edition? In the hushing up of this aspect of Marxist thought I detect a vein of political prudery whose motives – as almost always with prudery – are much more suspect than their target. My own attitude to Marxist military thought is quite different. The main criticism to which it lies open, in my belief, is that it is not developed systematically enough, not related clearly enough to the core principles of Marxist social and political theory. And this failure, I believe, has had damaging results for us all: a certain equivocation, a certain evasiveness in Marxist thinking in this area continues to this day to be a cause of genuine misunderstanding and unavoidable suspicion. But this said, I find much more to praise than to condemn in the specifically military thinking of the great Marxists. But before discussing this in any detail, I must say a little about the intellectual and political background against which this aspect of their thinking developed, and about the main reasons for which, in my belief, it deserves our careful attention.

Marxism, a unique amalgam of philosophical, economic, sociological and political theory, inspired by a vision of humanity liberated from age-old oppression by revolutionary means, came into existence in the mid-1840s. Everyone would agree that, on the one hand it draws its initial inspiration from the hopes and dreams of 1789 (and back of these from the perfectibilian doctrines of the Enlightenment), but equally that, from its first beginnings, Marxism stiffened and clarified these hopes and dreams, almost beyond recognition, by a new 'interpretation of history' and by original economic analyses of the working of the capitalist system. About the sources of this stiffening and clarification we need here notice one point only: they were, one and all, very recent intellectual achievements – certainly their influence did not become widespread until after 1815 – and taken together they strongly suggested that with the collapse of the Napoleonic adventure, an entirely new chapter in European history had begun. Despite their prodigious differences, Hegel's doctrine of the state, the analyses of Malthus and Ricardo, and the industrial sociology of St Simon and his disciples were alike in pointing mankind – or at least European men – back to their proper business after the twenty-five years of cataclysmic revolution and war. And that business was with *social* problems, that is, with problems that were bound to arise within *any* European state, and were also likely to spread across the borders of states, irrespective of their power or political traditions. To be sure, the so-called age of peace in which Marx and Engels grew up, contained foretastes of bitter, irreconcilable social divisions: new frenetic nationalisms and, in some countries, class-hatreds such as Europe had not known since the sixteenth century. But these dangers were beginning to be recognised as essentially social problems in the sense just described, and more specifically as results of the new social phenomenon of industrialisation. It was therefore not unnatural that, within three decades of Napoleon's fall, Marx and Engels should have been writing that all history is the history of class-struggles, and that during the same period Kant's deep concern with the problem of peace between nation-states should have seemed to most of his philosophical followers to have been a misplaced obsession. Problems of peace and war – so the harbingers of Marxism appeared to believe – would be met, in so far as they could be met, only when more basic social problems, transcending state-boundaries and conflicts, had been more or less satisfactorily settled. This presumption was so much part of the spirit of the age that Marx and Engels felt it unnecessary to spell it out explicitly in their earlier writings.

The tragedy of 1848, and more particularly the part played in it by Russian military might, and the successive diplomatic crises of the early 1850s, roused Marx and Engels from their youthful revolutionary dreams. The 1850s and 1860s were the decades which transformed Marxism from a strikingly contrived revolutionary manifesto into a solid body of theoretical and practical doctrine which – with the aid of some extraordinary pieces of good luck – was to change the political face of Europe and of the globe. They were also the decades of Marx's and Engels' prodigious feats of self-education, to the point of self-transformation: Marx becoming, in Schumpeter's phrase, the most learned of all great economists, while Engels, although remaining an effective pamphleteer on almost any social topic, turned himself into probably the most perceptive military critic of the nineteenth century.

Early in the 1850s he settled down to a thorough study of Clausewitz, Jomini, Willisen, and other military theorists. From Clausewitz he learnt to appreciate the continuity of political and military events and, more specifically, to recognise that in the nineteenth century not only could no war for great political stakes be fought without popular involvement, but that, conversely, such involvement was likely to be a forcing-house of social and political aspiration among the participants. Of equal importance, however, was his careful study of the American Civil War, undertaken in connection with weekly articles which he wrote for the British press, and which appeared over Marx's name. Engels was one of the first military theorists to see in this prodigious struggle – which most Europeans regarded as an amateurish colonial affair – signs of what must be expected in future wars between industrial societies: with the superiority of the defensive quite evident, and with economic pressures proving decisive in the end. But it was the triumph of Bismarck's militarism, and the suppression of the Commune by French government troops, which convinced the founders of Marxism that war and the preparation for war between the great European powers had become a subject of the first importance for the planners of the working-class revolutionary movement. During the last ten years of his life, Engels' ever active mind was divided between plans for exploiting the new military situation – caused by the creation of mass armies of newly enfranchised citizens – and deeper, saner forebodings in view of the arms race and alliances of the major European powers.

There is no need to pursue this thread of the Marxist saga further, just now. Suffice to say that Marxism, a revolutionary creed which had been conceived, and whose fundamental structure had been laid down, in an age of military quiescence (if not of genuine peace) came to political maturity and effectiveness some thirty years later in a Europe obviously dominated by the threat of total war. Hence, inevitably, a logically uneasy relationship between basic Marxist theory – with its emphasis on the long-term continuity of human socio-economic advances even though these were powered by incessant conflicts and crises – and the ever-sharpening recognition by Marxists of the intrusive and distorting effect which inter-state rivalries and wars were to play in the predicted transition from capitalism to socialism. Indeed, the real tragedy of Marxism, as I see it, does not lie with its inherent faults (which are many) or with the faults of the capitalist system which it sought to displace (which also are many), but rather in the fact that Marxist socialism, in the historical event, has come to confront Western capitalism less as its potential economic supplanter than as its rival for world military–industrial hegemony, a rivalry that is spurred on by a new version of the age-old suicidal quest for supremacy-for-the-sake-of-security-for-the-sake-of-survival.

But, if this is the case, what relevance, it may well be asked, have the classic writings of Marxism to our present concerns? If Marxism has been so tragically overtaken, and indeed nonplussed, by events, what relevance, what interest even can be found in those Marxist texts which reveal the awakening of its founders to the challenge – or the madness – of our classic century of war? My reply is as follows. Certainly if we were now to look to the classics of Marxism for positive guidance – or *a fortiori* for some panacea – to rescue us from our military anxieties and discouragements, we should be more than foolish. The time is long past, for even Marxists to look for practical salvation in the sacred books of that mid-nineteenth-century faith. But it is still possible to treat the great Marxists, at least in connection with our topic, as an educational benefit, and indeed as educators – if we contrast that word strongly with authorities, instructors, or guides. For in our field their worst intellectual faults can, curiously enough, be turned to our educational advantage. Because they have here no clearly and rigidly developed doctrine, their intellectual arrogance, their 'scientific' hubris, their frankly opportunistic interest in every aspect of the war-system of their day, serve as spurs to quicken thought, rather than as manacles to stifle it. If we are to enjoy this educational benefit, we must of course approach the classic Marxists with the appreciative view of the intellectual historian, not with the self-righteousness of vulgar hindsight. We must see them for what they were, in their dreams and deeds during the half century before 1914, without reference to later events whose final assessment is still far beyond our power. So, for a moment, let us remind ourselves of the kind of men they were, in their writing and in their deeds, during their most intellectually active years, rather than in terms of their grim political legacies.

They were of course revolutionaries; but revolutionaries of a quite special kind, conceivable only in their own time and place – nineteenth- and early twentieth-century Europe, and Germany and Russia in particular. They were fanatical – or if it be preferred, dedicated – revolutionaries; though I suspect they would, one and all, have disowned the latter epithet almost as vehemently as the former. They called themselves (following Engels' description of Marx) 'scientific socialists'. Would they, then, have claimed to be 'scientific revolutionaries?' To our ears the phrase is as absurd as it is ambiguous. Or would they have claimed to be professional revolutionaries? The phrase is this time unfairly pejorative. Yet the attributes 'scientific' and 'professional' do suggest an important part of their revolutionary character. The word 'scientific' here has no exact connotation; but it points to the fact that the classic Marxists envisaged their revolutionary goals and the main means to them in terms that would have been inconceivable before the scientific revolution of the seventeenth and eighteenth centuries, and would be equally inconceivable since the great crises and 'liberations' of physical science in our own century. They believed that their revolutionary programme conformed to certain very general laws which applied to the development and ultimate dissolution of every known politico-economic system, and to certain much more specific laws which applied to the development and future dissolution of the capitalist system in particular. This enabled them to present the kind of social change in which they believed so passionately as not simply in conformity with the laws of social dynamics, but as at once due to happen eventually in any event and – what was even more important – as capable of being expedited by appropriate human foresight, organisation and endeavour. This aspect of Marxist thought is familiar enough. What, however, of their 'professionalism'?

This is not so easily described or appreciated. Like all professionalism it was based, if not on established science, at least upon what its members believed to be the best relevant theory available; and like all professionalism it included a constant preoccupation with matters falling under its purview, with the attendant risk of seeing every event of importance from its own particular viewpoint (as lawyers, tend to see all important problems as legal problems, and similarly with politicians, engineers, doctors, etc.). This had the effect of making some of their comments – especially on bourgeois political issues – rather boringly predictable and childishly disparaging. But on other issues, notably those of war and peace between the European powers, their revolutionary concern, taken in conjunction with the would-be scientific framework of their thought, made them remarkably quick and often penetrating analysts of the political scene. Very few writers before them had ever tried to penetrate below the surface of international developments, or had achieved any notable success in predicting them. Marx and his immediate followers, however, armed with their overall theory of world development and with what they believed to be their theoretically complete insight into the development and decline of capitalist society, were able to produce confidently sweeping interpretations and assessments of every major diplomatic and military move on the European chessboard. Just as they were the first to treat capitalist crises and booms as signals of social and political unrest, so they were the first to present war or threats of war now as causes or catalysts of revolutionary activity, now as skilfully contrived moves by reactionary governments to forestall revolutionary unrest, now as desperate gambles between rival capitalist powers, now as tests which the revolutionary movements had to survive, and now as supplying the very agency – in the form of a mass citizen army – through which alone the existing order could be overthrown. And the fact that their revolutionary vision included, as one facet of its ultimate goal, the final achievement of a secure and genuine peace within and between co-operating socialist states, naturally added an irresistible attraction to their apparent all-knowingness, and the often remarkable shrewdness of their diagnoses and predictions.

Of course they were often wrong, utterly, disastrously, wrong: wrong in particular in their tendency to underestimate their opponents, from Bismarck to the founders of the British labour movement. But at least, because of the relative rigidity and comprehensiveness of Marxist social theory, their mistakes are usually of theoretical interest: they can be positively identified and corrected, and so can help us to think better than they did. More specifically, at a time when so many other social thinkers regarded military tasks and problems as a relic of a barbarous past, they at least saw the storm-clouds approaching and had a definite theory of their shape, their force and their direction. More generally, they were serious, they were students, and in their own fanatical way they were concerned; and by the standards of their age they – and in particular Engels – were extraordinarily well informed. And if, in their propaganda, they sometimes told lies about war, they certainly swallowed very few – at a time when most of their opponents were swallowing lies about war as if they were oysters.

It is against this background, and in this spirit of historical appreciation, that I now wish to consider the following groups of questions, which serve to indicate the main areas of Marxist concern with our topic.

(1) Does the Marxist theory of society aim, or claim, to explain the existence, development, and probable future of wars between human societies? And can any definite overall attitude, in the way of acceptance or rejection, limitation or elimination of war, be derived from – or indeed be properly expected from – the Marxist theory of society?

(2) What part, according to Marxist doctrine, must war *in the literal sense* be expected to play in any revolutionary takeover? For the founders of Marxism this usually meant in any revolution in an advanced industrial country. And within that context it is virtually equivalent to the question: how literally, with respect to such countries, must we take the phrase 'class-war'?

(3) Given that there have been many wars which have had no direct relevance to Marxist revolutionary aims, e.g. wars for European or for world hegemony from the sixteenth to the twentieth centuries, what should the Marxist attitude to future wars of this kind be? Should Marxists neglect them, spurn them, deplore and denounce them, boycott them or exploit them, endeavour to transform them, or what?

All these questions converge, in the treatment that follows, on the later political thought of Engels, which recent Marxist exegesis has tended to play down or neglect on some issues (perhaps because of its apparently German nationalist sympathies) and to misunderstand completely on others. In particular, we shall find that Engels' later views on the questions in our groups (2) and (3) above combine to give us one of the most important, although neglected, developments of classical Marxist thinking: the first, and by no means the last, socialist international policy aimed at forestalling the threat of world war. That the proposed policy had its weaknesses, and that Marxist parties in the two decades between Engels' death and the 1914–18 war failed completely to implement it, does not make it any the less deserving of careful and appreciative study.

As regards our first group of questions, the main difficulty is the lack of authoritative theoretical statements, which would show us the 'place' of war within the general Marxist theory of society. This lack, I believe, is not accidental: not simply a matter of Marx not having the time, or of Engels not having the philosophical force and skill to make it good. So let me make this claim more specific. If we look at any of the seemingly definitive accounts of 'the economic interpretations of history', i.e. well-known passages from the preface to *The Critique of Political Economy* from *Anti-Dühring*, from *Ludwig Feuerbach and the End of Classical German Philosophy* or from Engels' famous letter to J. Bloch of September 1890, we find that while such 'superstructural' activities as politics, the administration of justice, the arts and religion are placed, and said to be explainable, in relation to the fundamental productive powers and arrangements of different human societies, war is not referred to, in any of these writings, as being explainable in the same kind of way. And for this reason scholars who have sensed the logical gap that surrounds the notion of war in Marxist theory, have been driven to careful scrutiny and exposition of certain passages, none of them written with any great care or logical precision, in which Marx and Engels are evidently applying something that might be called 'the general Marxist position on war', but in which it is far from clear exactly what that position amounts to.

Can we offer a reconstruction of that position with any confidence that intelligent Marxists and non-Marxists alike could agree to it? Certain points at least can hardly be disputed. For the Marxists, as for Clausewitz before them, wars in different economic, technological and cultural epochs have meant very different things, and have produced profoundly different effects upon human history. And for this reason (among others) Marxism does not reject war in general as inherently evil or irrational: it approves of some wars, e.g. those fought to liberate suppressed classes and races, while disapproving of others that have an opposite purpose. (Nor, incidentally, does Marxism always find peace commendable: we may recall Marx's comments on the peace of economic stagnation which had persisted for centuries in the Orient.) But even more obviously Marxism finds nothing creative – or of positive human value – in war itself: according to Marxist theory human values arise from pressures for social change which rest, ultimately, on new possibilities of production; and it is only in so far as war helps to expedite such changes that it can be regarded as a progressive agency in human affairs.

Now these points, taken together, certainly suggest the view that war is intelligible only in relation to, and indeed as subordinate to, other deeper-lying changes in, and conflicts over, men's organisation of their productive powers. But is it subordinate to these changes in the same sense as politics, law, religion, etc. are said to be; namely, in Marx's words, as 'ideological forms' – modes of thought and action which partly express, partly disguise or distort, the basic economic divisions and changes which are, according to Marxism, the real motors of all human advance? Many Marxists seem to have believed that it is: and that, just as peace, as ordinarily understood, is, if not a sheer misnomer, at least a surface phenomenon cloaking persistent and occasional deadly conflicts, so also war, in the sense of war between nations, is not a phenomenon that can be studied or understood in any depth, except in the light of those deeper social conflicts which so-called peace so frequently conceals. In other words Marxism claims to explain war and peace, which are vulgarly regarded as ultimate opposites and alternatives, as calculable and gradable effects of deeper-lying changes in the ways in which societies organise their productive power.

In my belief there are strong reasons for doubting whether this can be true of all wars: more positively and specifically, there are strong reasons for maintaining that, even if all wars were caused in the way just indicated, *once begun* a good many wars develop in ways that cannot be explained by reference to deep, underlying economic conflicts and possibilities of change. (As we saw, in our discussion of Clausewitz, wars are liable to change in respect of their aims, methods and intensity as they proceed; and it is by their results – no matter how surprisingly or accidentally achieved – rather than by their causes or pretexts, that wars have left their main marks on history.) But this is not the point immediately at issue. What I now want to discuss is whether Marx and Engels in fact held anything like the 'general Marxist position in war' as I have just outlined it, and whether they adhered to that position consistently.

In trying to decide this question we could of course refer to countless arguments, dicta, slogans and asides from the corpus of their writings. But I think it will be both fair and sufficient to refer to three passages which have an unmistakably direct bearing upon it. The passages are from Engels' *Anti-Dühring* and *The Origin of the Family* and from Marx's *Grundrisse* (towards the end of notebook 4 and at the beginning of notebook 5). All three passages are concerned with the fact that in most known historical epochs, and in particular in the earliest chapters of European history, the political order has been determined, to all appearance, less by considerations of property and production than by considerations of a military nature – prevailing military needs and opportunities, military formations and command structures, together with the fruits of successful military campaigns. And, to a superficial reading, all three passages seem to be written to correct this impression and to prove that, despite the appearances, military factors have in fact been in all cases functionally subordinate to more basic, ultimately productive, factors in social life. Thus in the course of part 2 of *Anti-Dühring* (subtitled 'The Force Theory') Engels considers the social significance of war among, in particular, the earliest slave-based states of Ancient Greece.[2] The fundamental fact about these states, he maintains, is that in them human productive power had reached a crucial point of development – it was clear that considerable surpiuses could be accumulated if only the labour force could be drastically increased. The most readily available source of such now highly valued labour was through the enslavement of conquered foes. Hence the honoured position of war in the city-states of Greece; but hence equally the easily neglected truth that force, in this age (and contrary to the thesis of Herr Eugen Dühring), far from controlling society, was in fact 'pressed into the service of the social order'. Thus far, the argument is exactly on the lines that popular interpretation of Marxism would lead us to expect: war arises from basic social needs, and social arrangements of production, a general truth of which the latter-day expression has been the slogan 'Capitalism means war'. But in the course of his argument Engels remarks rather surprisingly that 'war was as old as the simultaneous existence alongside each other of several groups of communities'. In other words, the existence of war, as distinct from the social function here attributed to it, is postulated at the outset as an independent factor in the situation to be explained. War helps *in* – or *towards* – Engels' explanation of the economic development of the city-states, but is not itself explained by that development. Or, to be more exact, we are shown how war was used to advance certain economic purposes; but this presupposes its existence, as a permanent inter-societal possibility, independent of this or any other use of it.

The relevant passage from *The Origin of the Family* repeats and expands the pattern of argument which I have just expounded. Engels is here discussing the breakdown of the gens system of social organisation, which, following the American anthropologist L. H. Morgan, he believed to be the key to mankind's pre-political history. Pressure of population drove tribes to merge their separate territories into the aggregate territory of the nation, i.e. a social unit defined by the territory in its permanent possession. 'Thereupon war and the organisation for war became a regular function of national life...the wealth of neighbours excited the greed of nations...Pillage seemed easier and even more honourable than acquisition of wealth by labour. War, previously waged only in revenge for attacks or to extend territory which had become insufficient, was now carried on for the sake of pure pillage...and became a permanent branch of industry.'[3] Here again we should notice that the initial aim of the argument is to show the subordination of war to other more basic social needs and pressures. But we should also notice that not only is its independent existence, or the permanent possibility of its being activated, hinted at ('war, previously waged only in revenge for attacks') but, what is even more important, the inherent dynamism of war and its overwhelming attractiveness for large classes of men are now freely admitted (it 'was now carried on for the sake of pure pillage...and became a permanent branch of industry'). Now to admit the inherent dynamism of war, or, with Clausewitz, to recognise its inherently two-edged character, is in effect to abandon hope of explaining its development and effects within limits set by other more basic and productive social interests. Once again war appears to be as much an *explicans* as an *explicandum* in these far-off but crucial periods of human history.

Let us see how Marx deals with a closely connected question in the now well-known passage from *Grundrisse* referred to above. Here he discusses the rise of the early Mediterranean city-states of antiquity in which he finds the clue to all later Western forms of society. He puts forward an interesting sociological explanation of their incomparably high civic spirit – and of their equally unrivalled bellicosity; and he argues that it was their successes in war, resulting in a constant flow of slave labour, that eventually led to their replacement by the much less attractive slave-based societies of the Roman empire and the serf-based economy of Europe in the feudal age.[4] Marx's presentation of this thesis appears, at first, to conform entirely to the popular Marxist thesis that war, as an agent of social direction and change, is always subordinate to prevailing economic arrangements. At the dawn of Greek history, he tells us, we find, over the main Mediterranean area, tribes whose land-holdings had been in the past entirely communal, now coming together to form a new kind of polity. This was centred on a town or citadel, which was the symbol of communal defence and all community interests. But, as landholdings around the town were extended, so that some were physically very remote from others, a system of permanent private holdings for the purpose of cultivation grew up, and this in turn became a system of individual proprietorship by independent (mainly subsistence) farmers. The important point, however, was that independent ownership was endorsed and guaranteed by common recognition and communal defence. And indeed the needs of defence were to prove to be a kind of godsend: they gave a persistent and practical form to that city-based sense of unity without which the system of individual pro-prietorship could easily have led to disruption and anarchy. All this is conveyed, in the quaint telegraphese of *Grundrisse*, by such sentences as 'The survival of such a community means that its member families are reproduced as a self-sustaining peasantry, whose surplus time however goes to the community in the form of military service, i.e. the job of war.'[5]

Such in briefest outline is Marx's schematisation of early Greek and Roman history. The bellicosity of the great city-states is presented at once as a result of, and as an invaluable prop to, their remarkably balanced socio-economic organisation. But, just as in the Engels passages already discussed, so too here we find some curiously tell-tale comments. In his enthusiasm for the early city-state set-up Marx affirms that its 'difficulties could only arise from *other communities* [our italics] which have either previously occupied its land or which now wish to replace it as occupants'.[6] War, therefore, was not, so to speak, simply chosen as a way of life that would help to maintain civic unity: it was already there, at least potentially, from the outset, in the fact that the existence of one city-state means, almost inevitably, the existence of a number – an ever growing number of rival and probably hostile and warring states. Again when Marx writes of the early cities that 'War is the great common task, the great common labour which is required to perpetuate the occupation of the land which is the necessary condition of their liveli-hood together',[7] the greatness ascribed to this task is evidence of the fact that it is forced upon the citizens; it is not simply a fortunate prop to their civic unity, it is an independent factor in the situation, successful coping with which is necessary to secure that form of life, at once individual and intensely communal, which the citizens share and prize together. And the point comes out even more forcibly in the brilliant, better-than-Hegelian twist with which Marx ends this part of his argu-ment. He claims that it was the very success of the socio-economic *and military* set-up just described which led, dialectically, to its replacement by the social order of later antiquity. The independent farmer-warriors of the early city-states possessed an incomparable and irresistible civic and military morale: their successes in battle brought wealth of all kinds – tribute, slaves and vast new territories – to the most successful states. But this led, first in Athens in the fifth century and more signi-cantly in Rome from the third century BC onwards, to a socio-economic revolution, the arrival of a money economy, leading ultimately to the social fragmentation of the Roman Empire, with the greater part of production undertaken by slave labour, on the vast plantation-like *latefundiae*, with professionally enlisted armies defending and enforcing the peace, and with idle municipal rabbles replacing the independent farmers who had been held together by 'the great common task of war'.

My conclusion, therefore, is that in all three passages which we have examined, Marx and Engels, while paying lip service to something very close to what I have called the general Marxist position on war, are forced in the course of their analyses of concrete historical cases, to treat war and the permanent danger of war, in a much more commonsensical and indeed a much more illuminating way. They show us war and methods of war being profoundly influenced by other more constructive and creative forms of activity: but they also show us war conditioning and supporting these in the most surprising and lasting ways. In other words, they show us war as a relatively independent variable in the ever-changing human scene. And this view seems to me to be presupposed in many other passages in which Marx and Engels recognise the reality – and indeed the positive economic significance – of the main national divisions of modern Europe, and admit that such divisions are to be explained, not as the results of general economic forces, but as the results of particular wars through which the sense of nationhood has been cemented through the centuries.[8]

An adequate treatment of our second group of questions – how far revolution can be assimilated to regular war, how literally the phrase 'class-war' should be interpreted – ought perhaps to begin from a type of study which has recently been much in fashion, but which, surprisingly, has never been seriously applied to Marxist revolutionary teaching except in connection with its Hegelian ancestry. This type of study is focussed on the key terms in the vocabulary of a given movement or school of doctrine, and aims at bringing out clearly – and showing the main practical implications of – the main affinities and contrasting forces of these terms, and the main equivocations and hidden persuasions that they contain. Such a study is especially necessary, if also perhaps especially difficult, in the case of Marxist revolutionary doctrine, which was mainly forged in the correspondence of two friends, both of whom possessed brilliant powers of twisting traditional terms and concepts – in two languages – into new shapes and new relationships to assist their new theoretical preoccupations.

One of the principal uses of such a study would be to help us to decide what is sheer abstract rhetoric and what is figurative condensation of military fact and principle in a number of the writings of Marx and Engels. Consider for instance their claim, in the *Communist Manifesto*, to have traced out 'the more or less veiled civil war, raging within existing society, up to the point where the war breaks out into open revolution, and the violent overthrow of the bourgeoisie'.[9] In view of the seemingly non-consequential progress of this statement, must one assume that 'war' and 'civil war' are here being used in a to some degree metaphorical sense? Or what of the argument, to be found later in the *Manifesto*, that, in its struggles with the aristocracy, the bourgeoisie is forced to supply the proletariat with arms which the latter will then turn upon the hand that supplied them?[10] Here the immediate context explicitly suggests arms of an intellectual kind – in the form of political education – but the wider context suggests all the grim realities of armed struggle between the classes. Or again, how literally are we to take Engels' statement of some years later, that 'in politics there are only two decisive powers: organised state power, and the unorganised elementary power of the popular masses',[11] or Marx's insistence in his famous letter to Kugelman, on the need 'no longer to transfer the bureaucratic military machine from one set of hands to another, but rather to smash it. . .as the essential condition of every real revolution in the continent of Europe'.[12] It is easy to suggest the words and phrases with which a close study of this part of Marxist vocabulary should begin. The word which gives rise to the greatest difficulties is 'Gewalt', variably answering to the English words 'authority', 'might' and 'violence'. But a better starting point might well be the slide which we find in much Marxist theorising in our area, from 'Volkskrieg' (people's, or popularly backed, war) through 'Bürgerkrieg' (civil war) and 'Klassenkampf' (class combat or struggle) to 'Revolution' and 'Mass-empörung' (revolution and mass insurrection). In this connection Herr Blasius has pointed to two facts of considerable interest: first the eager acceptance, by both Engels and Lenin, of Clausewitz's virtual identification, within the early nineteenth-century context, of a people's or popularly backed war, with what he called Absolute War; and secondly their apparently wilful misinterpretation, or at least free extension, of Clausewitz's idea of a people's war to make it a natural stepping-stone to civil war and rebellion.[13] The different ways in which the Marxist leaders played – but never too fast or too loose – with the vocabulary and thought-patterns which they here took over from Clausewitz might well prove to be a rewarding line of study.

In urging the value of such a 'philological' approach to this part of Marxist doctrine, I am not suggesting or presupposing that Marx, Engels and Lenin – or any of their confrères – were either bad or careless or unusually confused or deceptive writers. The fact is simply that the way thinkers of any given school or tendency find themselves compelled to select, combine, reject or renew certain words or phrases is often an invaluable clue to the understanding of how other social influences and restrictions affected the development of their thought. And in the particular case of Marxist revolutionary doctrine, my guess is that such a study would reveal a steady clarification in their vocabulary – and hence in the analyses, prognoses and precepts with regard to the military aspect of revolution – from the early days of 1848, through the 1860s and 1870s, at least up to the death of Engels. For certainly, if I am right in the above general judgment, then it is in Engels' writings that such an improvement in Marxist thinking can best be traced out and appreciated. And this, I feel confident, is one of the main ways in which that enigmatic figure – so exuberantly energetic and many-sided yet curiously modest and shy, so touchingly tender and loyal in personal relations if occasionally coarse and brutal in intellectual judgements – will one day be rehabilitated by future historians of Marxism. For the last thirty odd years Marxist scholars have almost unfailingly marked Engels down as a mere journalist or misleading populariser of Marxist tenets. But in order to do justice to Engels there is no need to enter into comparisons between the two founding fathers of the movement: Marx was incomparably Engels' superior in economic learning and theoretical power, in philosophical originality and, as a writer, in his power of hammering home paradoxes until they are accepted as platitudes. Nevertheless Marx has left ample testimony to Engels' indispensable contribution to Marxist economics in the early days; and it is common knowledge that, on the educational side, Engels was the great teacher of German social democracy during the three crucial decades of its growth. What has still to be appreciated, however, is the significance, not only for Marxism during its heyday but for the general history of nineteenth-century civilisation, of Engels' military thinking during the last twenty years of his life. This related both to the military aspect of revolutionary activity as such, and to the interpretation of the military-diplomatic background against which such activity must be expected to take place. At this point I am concerned only with the first of these approaches.

Engels was not only a serious student of warfare and of war-theory, he had a positive relish for active military life. He had taken part in the South German uprising of 1849, eventually escaping to Switzerland and Italy, and always looked back on those months as an exciting, if somewhat disillusioning, holiday adventure. He was affectionately nick-named 'the General' by his friends; and he felt as directly drawn to military tasks and problems as to the other strangely varied passions of his life: to sociological and anthropological research, to hunting in the

English winters, and to the fighting Celtic spirit, as well as the beauty and freshness, of Irish working class girls. One of his first contributions to the military principles of revolution is to be found in the article which he wrote for the New York *Daily Tribune* in 1852, and which was later republished under the title *Germany: Revolution and Counter-revolution*. Here youthful enthusiasm predominates over careful reflection, although there is perhaps a trace of a hasty first reading of Clausewitz in the opening sentences.

Insurrection [he writes] is an art quite as much as war is...and is subject to certain rules neglect of which would be ruinous...First, never play with insurrection...it is a calculus with very indefinite magnitudes against forces that have all the advantages of organisation, discipline and authority...unless you bring strong odds against them, defeat and ruin are certain. Secondly, always act with the greatest determination and on the offensive. The defensive is the death of every armed rising...Surprise your antagonists while their forces are scattered, prepare new successes daily, keep up the ascendancy which initial success has given you...in the words of Danton, the greatest master of revolutionary policy yet known, 'de l'audace, de l'audace, encore de l'audace!'

This is fine rousing stuff, but its recommendation of persistent mass attacks upon well-armed troops is as remote from Clausewitz's tactical teaching as from the realities of nineteenth-century street-fighting. Face to face, line against line, a popular insurrection is seldom capable of beating down loyal and disciplined troops. Its characteristic posture – behind barricades – is plainly defensive, and its main weapons are psychological. Thus, if street barricades succeed in sealing off large areas of a city from the fire-power of government troops, the impression may well spread that government staffs and troops have been encircled and that outside aid will never get through to them. It is only at this stage, when officials and officers lose their nerve, that a mass attack upon some chosen centre may produce immense psychological effects. But the suggestion that such attacks should be kept up daily is absurd. For daily performance, the discipline and the routines of the armed forces have an incomparable advantage.

These are commonplace considerations. How could Engels, with his considerable military experience, have neglected them? The answer is suggested by the Danton quotation. It was the common belief – how far justified we need not argue here – that from 1789 to 1793 the populace of Paris had *made* the French Revolution, and that this achievement could always be repeated whenever the will was there, the prognosis scientific, the timing right and the organisation thorough.

But Engels' later military studies and appreciations – especially those, as already indicated, of the American Civil War, of Bismarck's wars, and of the suppression of the Commune – taught him better; and the main lessons he derived from these studies are clearly stated in his Introduction to the 1895 reissue of Marx's *Class Struggles in France*. Engels here recognises that all the weapons of an insurrectionary force – barricades, sorties, fraternisation with government troops, etc. – are primarily psychological. Their target has to be the morale, the discipline and the self-confidence of the government troops – and behind these of the government itself. The supreme fulfilment of every popular insurrection is that momentary vacuum which is caused by the flight, the disappearance or confessed non-competence of the government in being. Afterwards – with the picking up of the pieces – the endless confrontation with human realities begins again...But besides this general lesson, Engels pointed to a number of technical factors which had, in his belief, completely transformed, between 1848 and the 1890s, the possibilities of effective mass insurrection. First, the perfection of the railway system, which in most European countries now allowed reinforcements to be brought in overnight to almost any centre of disturbance: then the replacement of muzzle-loading rifles by breech-loaders, and of artillery round-shot and grape-shot by the new percussion-shells; and perhaps most important of all the wide streets and long regular tenements of the industrial suburbs of most great European cities, which could now be commanded, and in a few moments cleared, by cannon as never before. 'The revolutionary would have to be mad, who chose the working-class districts of North and East Berlin for a street-fight.'

This did not mean, however, that street-fighting and mass insurrection had no future role. While conditions had become far more favourable to the military, there would still be times and situations when a display of mass force would be indispensable – but at the climax rather than at the beginning of an uprising, and always in the light of what Engels refers to, in the Introduction of 1895, as 'other compensatory factors'. What he meant by this cautious phrase, can be gleaned by various writings of the same period. He meant first the advent of universal suffrage, then the rise to power of disciplined working-class parties and above all the general acceptance of military conscription, which in his belief had transformed completely the political environment in which future revolutionary uprisings could be expected. 'Contrary to appearances' he writes in 1891 with his mind particularly on Germany, compulsory military service surpasses general franchise as a democratic agency. The real strength of the German social democracy does not rest in the number of its voters, but in its soldiers. A voter one becomes at twenty-five, a soldier at twenty; and it is youth above all from which the party recruits its followers. By 1900 the army, once the most Prussian, the most reactionary element of the country, will be socialist in its majority as inescapably as fate.[14]

But what practical conclusions were to be drawn from these exciting suggestions? During the two decades between Engels' death and the outbreak of World War I most spokesmen of the radical wing of the German Social Democrat party accepted, on Engels' authority, that any successful revolution must in future depend on the co-operation of a majority of the nation's conscripted men. Engels wrote in a number of his later letters as if this conclusion had become so obvious as not to require further elaboration. For example, to Bebel in 1884: 'If the impulse [sc. to revolution] arises from Germany, then it can only start from the army. From the military point of view an unarmed nation against a modern army is a purely vanishing quantity.'[15] He then speculates on one of the politically most important consequences of 'our twenty to twenty-five years old reservists coming into action': with this new power behind revolutionary socialism 'the period of pure [sc. parliamentary] democracy might be skipped over...'.[16] But he nowhere explains how he envisaged a sufficient number of conscripts being indoctrinated, organised and directed as a revolutionary force, or for how long he supposed such a force would be needed to sustain a revolutionary régime. Engels' vagueness on these issues is understandable: Marxist political strategy has always insisted that the forms and methods of successful revolutionary action must be adapted to particular circumstances. On the other hand it is natural to argue that the apparently vague condition in which Engels left this part of his political legacy helps to explain the failure of the German Social Democrats and the French Workers' Party to take effective stands against the successive diplomatic crises that led to 1914.

The specific difficulties that here faced Engels have never, to my knowledge, been adequately appreciated in their tantalisingly delicate juxtapositions.[17] At first sight, the promise or prospect of a 'majority of socialists in the Prussian army' and of 'our twenty to twenty-five year old reservists coming into action' came as a godsend to Marxist political strategy. Already, in the 1880s, the idea of an irresistible uprising, driven forward by the continuous immiserisation of the masses, was beginning to lose credibility; while the one really promising European socialist movement, the German, owed its successes not to any revolutionary dreams or traditions, but to its admirable organisation, self-discipline and concentration upon the industrial demands of its members. In this situation the danger of political stagnation was real. On the other hand the promise of a majority of socialists in the Prussian army was as yet only a statistical trend: and one which carried, along with new hope for the Marxists, a worrying threat to the Prussian and other military autocracies. Moreover, it could easily turn out that the Prussian and other military autocracies were better placed and equipped to contain or direct the trend, than any Marxist social party was to exploit it. Indeed, unless it was exploited with great skill, the prospect or possibilities of a revolution spear-headed by the nation's conscripts might rebound on the German Social Democrats in either of two very unwelcome ways. The suggestion that they were planning or actually fomenting disaffection in the ranks of the army would provide the Prussian authorities with a perfect excuse for suppressing Socialist party activities even more harshly than Bismarck's Socialist Laws had done. And again, under the threat of disaffection in its army, any unstable government might well be tempted to re-establish its position by appeals to national unity and the defence of the fatherland against an alleged (or perhaps deliberately provoked) aggression.

But the difficulties involved in the idea of revolution by the soldiers were not confined to the probable reactions of governments. The idea of revolution in the form of a military uprising had no charms whatever for the leaders of German Social Democracy or of French socialist parties with their anarchist leanings. Bebel and the other German socialist leaders, with whom Engels established a close understanding in his later years, were neither fools nor cowards nor, contrary to widespread belief, men of narrowly economic outlook. But they had built up their party's organisation since the 1860s chiefly to improve the status – moral as well as material – of the German industrial working class. And they had espoused Marxism, and had secured at least formal acceptance of Marxism's goals and principles by their followers, largely because it promised to undercut, by methods as unexpected as they were irresistible, the ruthless dominance of their Prussian military rulers. It was the promise, hammered home in part 2 of *Anti-Dühring*, that all great social advances came about as a result *simply of economic causes*, which gave German Social Democracy its self-confidence, and within limits, its quality of heroic dedication. To be sure, all intelligent

Marxists knew that ruling classes will fight to hold on to their power after its economic basis has been cut from under them; but Marxism, as popularised in *Anti-Dühring*, had spread the belief that ultimate victory for the revolution was assured in advance, and that capitalism was destined to collapse from causes of its own creation, when all would be over bar the shouting, which would conveniently drown what little shooting had still to be done. And yet here was Engels, of all people, telling his devoted followers that, in the future, the success of any revolution must rest with the nation's conscripted soldiers. What was this but a recipe for civil war, in which the advantage must lie with those whose hands were on the levers of the great military machines, and whose determination to hold on to power in defence of their privileges was absolute?

Taken together, these difficulties no doubt help to explain Engels' silence about the actual preparation, methods and duration of a revolution spearheaded by the soldiers; but do they excuse it? Might he not here be accused of – to employ his own phrase – playing at insurrection, by holding out the prospect of an uprising, supported, if not led, by youthful social democrat conscripts, and yet failing to consider how this new trump card could best be played and the costs which playing it would involve? It seems to me, however, that, while the difficulties we have been discussing explain Engels' silence on this point, they explain it in a quite different way from that just suggested – and one which testifies altogether favourably to the wisdom and wiliness of his old age. We have to decide, in fact, whether Engels' concern with the role of conscripts in any future revolution was merely a last indulgence in his lifelong hobby of arm-chair strategy or was, on the contrary, an essential facet of a new and significant development of Marxist political thinking. As we shall see in a few moments, there is abundant evidence to show that the second of these alternatives is the correct one. Beyond question Engels in his last years saw his main political task as that of providing the German and French socialist parties with international and defence policies which were practically feasible, which took account of the ordinary German's and Frenchman's natural fears and patriotic feelings, and which would provide a possible escape-route from the threat of a general European war. At this point, however, what I want to explain is simply how Engels' concern with the revolutionary potential of modern conscript armies fitted into this ambitious political plan.

Sometime during the 1880s, it seems clear, Engels reached a momentous decision about the apparent or potential trump card which military conscription had put in the hands of European socialist parties. Contrary to natural expectation, the all-important task was not how to actualise it, but how to keep it potential – i.e. to use it, anyhow in the short-term, not as a lever of revolutionary change but simply as a justificatory idea, supporting and helping to explain a general socialist international policy. Of the considerations that led him to this view, only two need here be repeated: the resistance of the German Social Democrat to anything in the nature of an armed uprising, a repetition of 1848; and the equally evident menace of an utterly destructive European war. Both these considerations were putting a damper on the revolutionary impetus of the German Social Democrat movement; and Engels' immediate problem was how that impetus could be restored or replaced. His answer to it is found, not in any explicit reflections upon or defence of what he was doing, but in the main target of his political letters and newspaper articles, some of which were printed in all leading European languages, during the early 1890s, and especially after the Franco-Russian *accorde* of 1891. These letters and articles, tactful yet firm, persistent but never dictatorial, were aimed immediately – for Engels' ultimate revolutionary aims never varied – at an almost complete transformation in the outlook and efforts of the leading socialist parties of Europe. The socialist parties (especially the German Social Democrats and the French Workers' Party) had to proclaim themselves, or (to speak with effective modern vulgarity) had to 'sell' themselves, as the only parties worthy the name of 'party of national defence'. They must explain that they and only they were the natural and proper spokesmen for the great mass of the conscripts who would in fact fight and be killed in any 'defence of the fatherland'. And they must explain their right to speak and act as guardians of *their* conscripts in terms that could not be branded as treacherous or subversive by the ruling classes or as suicidally dangerous by the more timorous members of their own rank and file. They must show that they were completely sincere about the defence of their respective countries. French socialists must announce that they would resist invasion from any quarter – most obviously by German troops. German socialists must make it plain – within Germany and within France and Russia as well – that *they* would resist invasion from any quarter, would resist it to the death, whether in the form of French troops, of Russian troops or of both together. At the same time, the German Social Democratic parties must be prepared to argue that, besides being the only parties that could speak for their working-class conscripts, they were also the only parties whose defence policies meant something more than the preparation of an eventual European blood-bath. For, to socialist parties, defence must mean defence of the national soil not of the recent spoils of war (Alsace–Lorraine and Schleswig–Holstein) or of the current scramble for colonies.

In these ways the socialist parties of Europe (in particular of France and Germany) would build up for themselves positions of moral ascendancy, and indeed come to be regarded as their nation's natural defenders and rescuers in the event of a disastrous European war. At some point or other, whether at the beginning or at the end of an unpopular war, they would be in a position to take things over, with the overpowering support of their respective citizen armies. But in the meanwhile there was to be no talk of using conscripts for revolutionary purposes. This new trump card would do its work as an essential pillar, or precondition of a bold but (as I shall argue in a moment) by no means unrealisable international programme, by which socialist parties, hitherto so isolated and so outcast, would establish themselves as the parties of effective peace-making and peace-keeping. But in order to pursue this topic further we must turn back, briefly, to our third group of questions, dealing with possible Marxist reaction to wars for political hegemony or for commercial and colonial predominance between the great European powers.

Marx's and Engels' serious interest in these questions dated from the 1850s, when they first outlined what might be called a military sociology of governments and peoples. The purpose of this study was to determine both the susceptibility of different governments and peoples to the temptation of war, and, equally, the vulnerability of different governments and peoples to the actual experience of war. From the former point of view autocratic governments were always to be mistrusted – this echoed the opinion of many eighteenth-century thinkers, including Rousseau and Kant – and on this score Tsarist Russia was always the Marxists' prime enemy, with Bismarck's Prussia and Louis Napoleon's France vying for second place. All these, but especially Tsarist Russia, needed war. Bismarck and Napoleon needed successful wars to maintain their ill-founded régimes at particularly difficult moments. But with Tsarism the necessity of war had both a much simpler and also a much more sinister explanation. War was the one means by which Tsarist Russia could extend its own interests: and, among these interests, perhaps the most important was that no notable constitutional or economic reform should be made by its immediate neighbours, lest these should arouse similar aspirations within Russia. On the other hand, as between inherently militaristic governments, there were great differences in respect of their vulnerability to the experience of war. Marx and Engels took it for granted that Russia, under virtually any form of government, was secure from foreign conquest. Therefore, if Tsarism was ever to be dislodged from its position as the gaoler of Europe, this must come about through revolution from inside Russia itself. And hence, the almost extravagant hopes which Marx and Engels placed, in their later years, upon Russian revolutionary groups, Populist as well as Marxist. By contrast they always maintained (rightly) that the French Second Empire, and (much more questionably) that Bismarck's Prussia, would collapse at the first suggestion of military difficulties, let alone outright military defeat: whereas – yet another contrast – they perceived that the British (or, as they always said, the English) political establishment, being much more securely grounded, could be relied upon to keep out of potentially suicidal wars.

Turning now from governments to peoples, we must bear in mind that, for Marx and Engels, the real interests of any nineteenth-century European people were centred on those of its organised, potentially revolutionary, working class. Given this assumption, it was natural that their attention should have been focussed, from the early 1850s onwards, on the attitudes to war and to international relations generally, of the working-class movements of Germany and France. (They appreciated that in the very long run, social developments in America and Russia might here be of decisive importance; but, in the short term, what would happen in either of these as yet undeveloped countries seemed to them as unpredictable as what was happening in England always seemed to them exceptional). Marx and Engels were often critical, and sometimes all but despairing, of the socialist parties of France and Germany; and their attitudes to their leaders and programmes varied frequently and sometimes overnight with changes in the European military and political scene. All that I am now concerned with, however, is whether such changes of attitude rested on any single and consistent line of international strategy. This question is not carpingly put: nor is it a matter of mere academic interest. For it leads straight into one of the most bitterly problematic areas in the whole of Marxist exegesis: namely the doctrinal split on the issues of war and peace, which was to develop in the first two decades of our century between the leaders of, in particular, German Social Democracy on the one side and Lenin and his tiny group of followers on the other. I want here to discuss one aspect of this fateful division which I think has never received sufficiently clear-headed treatment: namely the degree to which it can be traced to, and to which blame for it can be imputed to, the teachings of Engels during the last ten years of his life. This question, it seems to me, is of great importance, not only for the understanding of Marxism at a crucial phase of its development, but more generally for any theoretical, or at least comparative, study of international relations.

A seemingly strong case for a continuous and consistent Marxist international strategy could be made out as follows. From the early 1850s, Marx and Engels always regarded the threat or actual outbreak of a major European war from one simple point of view: it might provide the opportunity, or act as the catalyst for, an effective revolutionary uprising, aimed at the ultimate liberation of the masses, even if its short-term objective had to be of a more prosaically limited kind. From this point of view Lenin's lonely stand in 1914 – his flabbergasting demand that socialists of all countries should work for the defeat of their *own* countries in order to exploit the fratricidal struggle for the sake of the general socialist cause – was only an extreme form of what had always been the accepted Marxist doctrine: and it could well be argued that this extreme strategy was needed to match the extremity of the occasion. This thesis, developed polemically against almost the entire leadership of the German Social Democrat Party and the French Parti Ouvrier after August 1914, has of course long since become encrusted in Marxist Leninist orthodoxy. Its weakness, however, is that it ignores the sources, motives, developments and difficulties which led to and largely explain, even if they do not excuse, the political ineptitudes and near-paralysis of the leaders of the German and French socialist parties at the outbreak of World War I. The thread of continuity in Marxist revolutionary strategy was not suddenly snapped by treacherous hands: it had begun to fray and to show signs of unravelling nearly thirty years earlier, at the hands, not of regressive nationalists or revisionists in the Marxist camp, but of the man whom Lenin, as much as the French and German socialist leaders, regarded as their great political teacher: namely Engels. For it was he who first raised doubts about the assumption that European wars could be regarded merely as springboards for socialist revolution. How, why and to what extent had he done this?

We have already seen Engels' thought drifting in what might have seeemed a dangerously nationalist direction, over the question of military, and in particular of conscript, participation in any future revolution; and, in close connection with this, in his insistence that the different European socialist parties, particularly those of France and Germany, must learn to present themselves as the only genuine parties of national defence. Of course this apparent concession to traditional national feelings was to be balanced, in Engels' plan, by an equally powerful insistence that the different European socialist parties enjoyed a unique relation to each other – having no essentially conflicting economic aims and hence no endemic mutual suspicions and rivalries. But this daringly paradoxical plan – or sketch of a political strategy – did not spring simply from, and did not simply give brilliantly impertinent expression to, the idea that socialist parties were becoming the natural and proper spokesmen of the different national armies of Europe. Behind it, and contributing massively to its potential appeal, was a recognition of the age-old if ever-ineffective belief that wars as such – and especially wars between the powerfully armed European nations – were a terrible evil, which must be forestalled or at least contained so far as the basic divisions of human society allowed. This was a notable change from the idea of war as primarily, or on Marxist principles, a useful springboard for revolutionary action. And we may well ask what had caused Engels to give new attention, even if belatedly, to so simple – some might have thought, to so jejune – a point of view. Was it the humane wisdom – or was it the cerebral softening – of old age? Had Marx's death, and his replacement by younger, mainly German Social Democrat confidantes, already begun to affect the main tenor of Engels' political thinking? These questions call for a wider study of the relevant sources than I have been able to give to them. But my own inclination is towards a quite different explanation. For over thirty years Engels had been a close student of European (and of American) military developments. As always, he had had no difficulty in drawing from these studies a number of useful, if not theoretically central, lessons for Marxist revolutionary strategy. But now, it seems natural to assume, a number of larger and simpler conclusions from these years of military study were beginning to exert pressure on the main thrusts of his political thinking, while at the same time – from the mid-1880s onwards – the European arms race, the increasing manpower requirements of the great powers, the successive diplomatic crises and the division of Europe into two armed camps, were giving these large and simple conclusions a more-than-revolutionary urgency. Engels was by no means the only political thinker of the period to be alarmed by these developments. But I would claim that no one else in his time envisaged as he did the *totality* of what we have come to call 'total war'.

Here are a few specimen passages from his later notes, letters, newspaper articles, etc. First, on the arms race, a note from the 1880s: 'Peace continues only because the technique of armaments is constantly developing, consequently no one is ever prepared; all parties tremble at the thought of world war – which is in fact the only possibility – with its absolutely incalculable results.'[18] Then, on the political and social consequences of a general European war, these two passages from letters, the first – to Bebel – dating from 1882. 'This time war would be terribly serious: it would set jingoism going everywhere for years, because every nation would be fighting for its very existence. All the work of the revolutionary in Russia would be rendered useless; our party in Germany would be swamped and ruined by the flood of jingoism, and it would be the same in France.'[19] Six years later he wrote to Sorge on the same theme, but with a more definite stress on the social consequences: 'A war, on the other hand, would throw us back for years. Chauvinism would swamp everything...Germany would put about five million armed men in to the field, or ten per cent of the population, the others about four or five per cent, Russia relatively less. But there would be from ten to fifteen million combatants. I should like to see how they are to be fed; it would be a devastation like the Thirty Years' War. And no quick decision could be arrived at, despite the colossal fighting forces...'[20] And finally a more comprehensive and horrific statement from Engels' preface to a work of military history published in 1888:

No war is any longer possible for Prussia–Germany except a world war and a world war indeed of an extension and violence hitherto undreamt of. Eight to ten millions of soldiers will mutually massacre one another and in doing so devour the whole of Europe until they have stripped it barer than any swarm of locusts has ever done. The devastations of the Thirty Years' War will be compressed into three or four years, and spread over the whole Continent. We will see famine, pestilence, general demoralisation both of the armies and of the mass of the people; hopeless confusion of our artificial machinery in trade, industry and credit, ending in general bankruptcy; collapse of the old states and their traditional state wisdom to such an extent that crowns will roll by dozens on the pavement and there will be nobody to pick them up; absolute impossibility of foreseeing how it will all end and who will come out of the struggle as victor; only one result is absolutely certain: general exhaustion and the establishment of the conditions for the ultimate victory of the working class. This is the prospect before us when the system of outbidding in armaments is driven to extremities, and at last bears its inevitable fruit.[21]

In these passages the main consequences of World War I, although not of course the technical means which it employed, is foretold with remarkable precision. The one false note is the mechanically dutiful claim that the condition of utter exhaustion and demoralisation portrayed in the last passage must make for the ultimate victory of the working class. But what was the practical import of Engels' predictions? Did they signify – did he intend them to suggest – a definite break with the previous Marxist view of European wars as primarily opportunities for revolutionary upheaval? To answer these questions we must revert, briefly, to our earlier discussion of the general Marxist view of the role of war in human history and of the ambiguity which Marx's and Engels' applications and illustrations of that view betray. It certainly seems as if, here again, Engels, when confronted with a live historic issue, was forced to recognise that war is a social force having an inherent dynamism of its own; a force which, whatever its causes, can produce effects which show no definite relation of dependence upon the main pattern of mankind's economic advance. This being so, the existence and permanent possibility of war calls for political treatment which, while evidently not independent of the economic changes upon which Marxist theory is centred, certainly cannot be derived from – or prescribed as a necessary part or aspect of – the core of Marxist teaching. But rather than re-argue this point of abstract doctrine, it will be more useful here to consider the specific practical proposals through which Engels strove to articulate and communicate his concern with the menace of general European war.

As we have seen, Engels was convinced that the one way in which socialist parties could forestall such a war was by developing and vigorously proclaiming an international policy of their own. What should the ingredients of such a policy be? Engels wisely insisted that the different national circumstances of the different socialist parties must be considered: and that the relatively peaceful tactics which he recommended for contemporary Germany could not be followed in France, Belgium or Italy. In Germany, however, the primary task for the Social Democrats was to establish themselves in the public mind (and to establish a corresponding self-image of themselves) as a party bristling with constructive ideas, well armed with arguments and ready to bargain realistically on the supreme issue of national defence. Engels seems to have sensed, in advance, the fatal weakness which, more than anything else, explained the failure of the German Social Democrats in the coming decades: their satisfaction with a posture of self-righteous protest, illustrated in a carping attitude – without positive alternatives – on war-credits, and in a strange passiveness – although very far from thorough-going pacifism – in the face of the drift to war. To counter this weakness, Engels came forward with proposals which today, after the disillusioning history of our century, may have come to sound hollow, but which in the early 1890s, when the great technicalisation of warfare had hardly begun, were much more realistic. The Social Democrats should not vote against defence credits so long as Russia continued to rearm; on the other hand they should persistently argue that additional credits should be offered exclusively for the *defence* needs for which they were requested. This position must then be shown to dove-tail with two others. Since Prussia had begun the arms race, and her system of recruitment was being copied by all the major powers, she should now take the lead in a sane programme of disarmament: a gradual diminution of the term of military service could easily be effected by international agreement, and this in turn should be used by Prussia to institute (again a gradual) transition from the regular army to some form of militia system. In 1893 Engels published a series of articles in *Vorwärts*, entitled 'Can Europe disarm?', in which he expanded these proposals, emphasising the political and financial advantages of a militia system, organised on the basis of local defence needs and making use of the entire male youth of the country on the Swiss model. The purpose of his articles, he wrote, was to do all in his power to prevent 'the general war of annihilation'. He was therefore confining himself 'to changes which are possible at the moment. . .I am limiting myself to such changes as any existing government can accept without endangering the security of its country. . .' And he concluded: 'From the purely military point of view there is nothing to prevent the gradual abolition of the regular army; and if the regular army *is* still maintained, it is maintained not for military but for political reasons – in a word, it is meant for defence, not against a foreign enemy, but against a domestic one.'[22]

But no matter how cogent Engels' arguments, we all know that they came to nothing. Whatever else German Social Democracy may have achieved during the next twenty years, it did not produce or sustain an effective socialist international policy. The fault was in part Engels' own. He had, no doubt, tried to pull off too much – to foist upon the Social Democrat leaders a policy stance which appealed hugely to *him* but which aroused in *them* all manner of misgivings and defeatist anxieties in the face of a world of which they knew nothing but feared so much – the world of secret diplomacy, of telegrams and armament deals, and of terrible decisions callously taken. As early as 1891 Bebel had criticised Engels' ideas on the ground that they would be unintelligible to German parliamentarians and military chiefs.[23] And to this we must add that to have won the Social Democrat rank and file to a whole-hearted support of Engels' plan, and to have kept that plan constantly before the minds of the German electorate, would have called for persuasive and organisational gifts of an unusually high order. The only European publicist of the pre-1914 age who came near to popularising Engels' views was Jaurès, whose book (*Armée Nouvelle* published 1910) repeated Engels' central claim that, if all western powers would settle for armies of the militia type, it should be possible to combine effective national defence measures with the reasonable hope that war would never again be necessary. But Jaurès' book was at once accused of pro-Germanism and failed to win over the majority of French socialists, let alone French public opinion at large.

There were, however, other reasons why Engels' ideas should have failed to inspire an effective international socialist crusade. There were rival socialist doctrines in the field, which, although never widely accepted before 1914, nevertheless indicated significant changes in feeling, outlook and preferred modes of action among the most active subgroups of the Second International. The first to make its mark was the militant pacifism – a policy of internationally organised strike action in the event of war – advocated by the Dutch socialist leader, Domela Nieuwenhuis. Domela attacked what he called Bebel's policy (in fact Engels' policy) at what was its boldest and, at the same time, its most vulnerable spot. The hope of rechannelling traditional national sentiments into the vigorous support of non-aggressive militia forces could not be squared with one of the most deeply entrenched of Marxist beliefs: that the main threat to European socialism lay in Russian military might. In the event of a Russian attack on Germany, Domela argued in 1892, 'French socialist workers will march shoulder to shoulder against German socialist workers: they, on their side, will be marshalled in their regiments to murder their French brothers. . . Whether we are applauded or not, whether we are called anarchists or what you will,

we declare that those who agree with Bebel are fostering jingo sentiments and are far from the principle of internationalism.'[24] The only
effective way of stopping wars was for socialist parties and trade unions
in all countries to commit themselves in advance to a general strike, and
for socialist conscripts to refuse to serve at the outbreak of war. Domela
was an ex-Protestant pastor, who later – and not surprisingly – became
an anarchist. His speeches at the early conferences of the Second International were brushed aside as cranky to the point of being simple-
minded by all the leaders of Marxist socialism – Bebel, Adler, Guesde
and Plechanov, as well as Engels. But to a considerable number of
socialists who read or heard him, Domela's ideas had the attraction of a
heroic simplicity. He pointed to what, in his belief, had to be done –
and had to be expected and risked – *absolutely*; whereas, in Engels'
plan, everything was conditional upon the results (or prospective results)
of elections, upon the success of parliamentary campaigns, as well as
upon developments in the immensely complex diplomatic and military
scene. In short, Domela's alternative exposed the excessive intellectual-
ism – the lack of a simple core of urgent, unconditional appeal – in
Engels' carefully balanced counter to the menace of European war.
It is not surprising, therefore, that his main contentions should have
been long remembered and should have reappeared, again and again,
in the later history of the Second International – in Gustave Hervé's
bitterly anti-patriotic propaganda, for instance, and even in some of
the revolutionary tactics of Rosa Luxemberg. But by the time these
revivals were under way, a second and much more important challenge
to Engels' anti-war policy – or rather to what German Social Democracy had made of Engels' anti-war policy – had come from the east:
from the relatively small Russian socialist party headed by Lenin.

Lenin's lonely but, in the end, world-confounding, stand against the
1914 war has been explained (by himself and by his followers) as a
simple act of Marxist consistency and courage. He, virtually alone
among the acknowledged socialist leaders of the time, stood by the
teaching of Marx and Engels, that every 'capitalist war' must be considered simply as an opportunity for advancing the cause of internationalist socialism. All the others, the Kantskys, the Guesdes, the
Plechanovs – Bebel and Jaurès now being dead – turned their backs on
this simple truth: Lenin alone had the intellectual and political tenacity
and the personal courage to stand by it. And thereby, out of his complete isolation, he was to become the one unquestionably 'world-

historical individual' of our century. At the same time the schoolmaster in Lenin assisted the revolutionary hero in castigating the unhappy backsliders in a manner that admitted neither recovery nor forgiveness. He presented them, in his polemics, not simply as traitors, but as ignoramuses – almost as buffoons. Had they read nothing, or forgotten everything they had ever read? Had they forgotten their own pledges in the Basel Manifesto of 1912? Had they never heard that war was simply a continuation of politics by other means; and that the first duty of every statesman, in the face of any war, was to determine its political character, i.e. what it was intended to achieve?[25] From the lambastings which they received in *The Collapse of the Second International* (summer 1915) and *Socialism and War* (August of the same year) the betrayers of Marxism could never recover, either in action or in historic repute: they had been thrown 'out of the history' by the man who was destined to command its future developments.

Such has long since become the established Marxist–Leninist view. But it requires no great historical erudition or prolonged doctrinal wrangling to demonstrate that things were not quite as simple as Lenin and his followers have made them out to be. Fifty years after his death it is widely accepted that Lenin was primarily a man of action, and as such liked to have his principles, i.e. his *Marxist* principles, cut and dried, simple and rigid – like so many levers and brakes and warning signals to assist his prodigious revolutionary undertaking – but also dispensable if they should fail to meet his requirements. Engels' later thoughts and plans for the prevention of a disastrous European war were an example of the last point. I have not found any passages in which Lenin explicitly rejected them: indeed it is quite possible that he did not know of their existence. What is quite clear, however, is that he would have had no use for them, even if he had admired them as examples of political appreciation and propaganda. They had simply no bearing on *his* problems. Still less had the difficulties and shocks and disappointments which help to explain the tragic failure of German and French socialism, on international issues, after Engels' death. These antecedents of the débâcle of August 1914 were also 'out of the history'.

To be fair to Lenin, we must specify this thesis a little more precisely. At least up till 1917 Lenin largely was, and certainly wanted to be, and equally *needed to be*, an orthodox Marxist. When, some years before 1914, he began to interest himself in international questions, he took over, unquestionably, the Marxist assumption that the coming revolution must take place in a *number* of the most industrially developed European nations. But Lenin's particular job – whose particularity need not be imputed to any narrow nationalist feelings – was always to promote the revolution in Russia. And this being the target of all his efforts, he naturally tended to regard revolutions in other countries, and still more a cataclysmic war between the great European powers, as so many aids to the fulfilment of his personal task. For, contrary to Marx and Engels, who had maintained that Tsarism would fall only to a revolution from within, Lenin was persuaded that it would fall only as a result of an utterly disastrous war – and that meant as long a war, and as generalised or global a war, as possible. (This helps us to understand the anxiety which he sometimes expressed, lest World War I might end too soon, before it had been adequately 'used' to speed up the collapse of capitalism.) In sum, Lenin's stance in 1914 was not simply good Marxism, a faithful adherence to its classic teachings (as found particularly in *Civil War in France*, with Engels' introduction to the 1891 edition, and recently reaffirmed in the Basel Manifesto of 1912); it was also a necessity of his particular task as leader of the majority party of the Russian Marxist Socialists. It would have been as impossible – or at least as politically suicidal – for Lenin to have abandoned that stance in August 1914, as it would have been for the German Social Democrats to have declared themselves enemies of their own government, and have pledged themselves to work for its defeat in the impending war. Lenin was committed, in fact if not in word, to international socialism *for the sake of one country*, from 1911 onwards, if not from the outset of his revolutionary career.

But is not this simply to say that, like all 'world-historical individuals' Lenin's political achievements were infinitely greater, judged in the light of history, than his own conception of his role could possibly have suggested – to himself or to anyone else? For who could possibly have foreseen that the fulfilment of Lenin's primary aim – the collapse of Tsardom in conditions of total social disintegration and military defencelessness – should have paved the way to the Soviet Union's emergence as one of the two superpowers of the later twentieth century? This brings us to two further, closely connected questions. How is Lenin's political triumph – even if it first became plain many years after his death – to be accounted for? And does that triumph mean that he, Lenin, was completely and finally right in his reversion to a simplistic Marxist view of war, while Engels, with his concern to prevent, or at least to shorten or contain, a general European war, was completely and fundamentally wrong?

An adequate answer to the first question would have to take note of factors which could not possibly have been appreciated by Lenin, and which have been either ignored or strangely mis-described by later Marxist theorists and historians: as that World War I, which did its work so well for Lenin's purpose by speeding up the collapse of capitalism in Russia, also dealt a less immediately obvious, but in the end highly significant, blow to the economic dynamism and political self-confidence of the capitalist powers of the west; and that the increasingly 'total' character of modern warfare (at least up to 1945) made Russia's vast spaces, and vast resources in manpower, an even greater asset than previous history could have suggested. For an adequate answer to our second question, we must look beyond the historic record to date, which admittedly shows an overwhelming balance in favour of Lenin. Engels, however, had recognised, in his practice, the existence of a problem which Lenin had never appreciated, which Stalin was no doubt congenitally incapable of appreciating, but which later rulers of Russia would appear to have recognised, if only intermittently, and without wishing to seem over-impressed by it. This problem arises – to repeat my previous assertion – from the fact that the existence of war, and its today ever more incalculable destructive effects, cannot be considered or dealt with or controlled, simply as one facet or by-product of mankind's great constructive task of achieving a just and satisfying economic order. Or to speak more simply, from its first beginnings Marxist overall social theory was defective, through its failure to place and explain the different possible roles of war in human history. That Lenin should have been proved right in action, while ignoring this defect, and that Engels, in endeavouring to make it good, was partly responsible for the tragic failures of German Social Democracy, does not mean that Lenin was altogether right, and Engels altogether wrong. On the contrary, the capacity of any theorist to notice, even if he cannot effectively settle, large outstanding difficulties, is one that will in the end win recognition, wherever standards deserving the name 'scientific' continue to guide human endeavour.

# 5

## TOLSTOY:
## FROM 'WAR AND PEACE' TO 'THE
## KINGDOM OF GOD IS WITHIN YOU'

Tolstoy's concern with war falls, at first sight, into two sharply contrasting stages. In his wayward youth and immensely creative early middle age, his literary response to war, as to all other great excitements and trials of life, showed a remarkable width and depth of feeling, perception and judgment. To this stage belong his masterly journalistic sketches of the fighting at Sebastopol, his early tales of army life, and the epic accounts of battles and campaigns in *War and Peace* – to the last of which he appended his often less happy diatribes against the 'great men' theory of history. There followed the period of Tolstoy's spiritual and nervous crisis, from which, he believed, he had been saved only by his conversion to his own idiosyncratic version of Christianity, centred on the command 'Resist not him that is evil.' This, it is natural to infer, explains his later concern with war which was certainly not the result of any new experience of it nor of further study and reflection on its role in history, but rather of some private psychological necessity. And what else could this necessity be but his continuous struggle, during his last thirty years, to live by – and to present himself as at peace with – his new Christian vision, which implied the total rejection of war? This, it is widely believed, was the inspiration of such fiercely polemical essays as *Christianity and Pacifism* and *The Kingdom of God is within you*.

Both stages of Tolstoy's thought about war have been subjected to careful study by biographers and literary critics, as well as by historians of ideas and spokesmen of different pacifist movements. But, to my knowledge, no one has thought it worth while to ask whether there might not be an important continuity between them. More particularly, the philosophical disquisitions which bulk larger and larger as *War and*

*Peace* proceeds, have usually been regarded as so much metaphysics –
so many attempts to show how far, or rather how little, wars can be
*understood* at all. No attempt, to my knowledge, has been made to see
the connection between these passages and, on the one hand, the one
justification of war which Tolstoy offers in *War and Peace* and, on the
other hand, the actually anti-patriotic positions which he advocates in
his later essays. Of course there are causes, and indeed excuses, for this
lack of interest. It is not at all easy to grasp all the different threads of
thought which Tolstoy was pursuing (and in some cases initiating) in
the philosophical chapters of *War and Peace*; so that, while severe
criticisms of these passages have been two a penny since *War and Peace*
first appeared, no one – again to my knowledge – has seriously considered the question: what are the offending passages doing in the
novel at all? or, more positively, how, despite their manifest weaknesses,
are they organically related to the main message of the novel? But the
most important cause for this strange lack of interest is much simpler:
it is that, apart from his pacifist disciples, few of Tolstoy's exponents
and critics have treated his later anti-war essays with the seriousness
they deserve. As with his ventures into aesthetics, economics, educational theory and Christian theology, so in our field, comfortably
established *cognoscenti* have assumed that Tolstoy's occasional gaffes
– individual errors of judgment – provide an excuse for not pondering
carefully the bold, pertinent and extremely uncomfortable truths which
the best of his later writings contain. I shall therefore be concerned in
this chapter to show not only that there is one important continuity of
thought on questions of war and peace from Tolstoy's earliest to his
latest writings, but that, among these, *Christianity and Pacifism* and
*The Kingdom of God is within you* deserve to be ranked among the
classics of anti-militarist (rather than of effective pacifist) literature.

Throughout his writing life Tolstoy was more concerned with the *truth*
and *falsity*, than with the heroism and horror, the excusableness or
sinfulness, of war. We find a striking, if excessively fulsome, expression
of this in the closing paragraphs of part 2 of *Sebastopol* – that brilliant
anticipation of the front line journalism of our day – where he writes

Perhaps what I am saying here is one of those evil truths which should
never be uttered, but should be kept hidden unconscious in each man's
soul, lest they prove hurtful...For who is the villain, and who the hero of
my story? *All* [and he then lists the names of some of the individuals whose
behaviour under fire he has just been describing]...'all are good, and all

are evil... The hero of my story, whom I love with all the energy of my soul, and whom I have tried to set forth in his full beauty is – The Truth.

But what was this far from attractive young man – intolerably arrogant, markedly unreliable, morbidly self-absorbed – able to contribute to our grasp of the truth of war? It will be useful to answer this, not specifically in terms of his Sebastopol sketches, but more generally, in terms of one feature of Tolstoy's method and skill as a novelist, which is of the first importance for assessing his achievements and failings as a philosopher of war and peace as well as an anti-war propagandist.

Like all genuine novelists Tolstoy excelled in presenting imaginary individuals, scenes, human conflict and continuities, in ways that completely engage the reader's interest and feelings. But more important for our present purpose is his mastery of what I will call explanatory comment. While reading Tolstoy, we do not simply feel, see and hear the life that he describes: we feel assured, we are wholly persuaded, that this is the way things go, that what he is telling us is completely true to life, even when he is describing situations of a kind we could not possibly have experienced. This is, in large measure, due to the apparently casual comments which he slides in, as if they were parentheses in his dialogues and descriptions of action, with an extraordinary confidence and skill. I don't think this part of Tolstoy's mastery requires or admits of further analysis or explanation, although the well-known theory of the division between his Russian sensibility and his French-trained critical intellect may help to illuminate it. But be this as it may, what matters to us is that from early manhood to old age – from *Childhood* written when he was twenty-three to *Hadji Murad* published after his death – he had simply to bend to the task of direct descriptive writing, and lo! there streamed from his pen not only scenes of incomparable vividness and power, but, in the closest and most natural relation to these, phrases, sentences and paragraphs of intellectual guidance – assuring, reminding, alerting his readers, explaining, classifying and de-mystifying the most critical shifts and developments in his narrative and characterisation – to an extent and with a consistent skill that we find in no other novelist. Two aspects of this peculiar mastery are especially relevant to Tolstoy's concern with the truth of war, as we find it most fully expressed in the descriptions, critical comments and philosophical disquisition of *War and Peace*.

First, let me try to suggest, very roughly, the predominant logical character of his explanatory comments. Several critics have remarked how often these are *behavioural*: this, he tells us, is how soldiers learn to overcome fear, or how men learn to comport themselves in different social situations; this is what the very old look for in everyday life, etc. But Tolstoy's explanatory comments are the exact opposite of those behaviourist explanations which claim to provide sufficient causes for different forms of human reaction. Unlike these – and this is a great proof of Tolstoy's novelistic wisdom – he is content to remind us that, despite appearances to the contrary, this is how such and such a group of human beings tend to behave within a fairly clearly marked range of circumstances. The purpose of the comment is to show that some particular development in his narrative is not only dramatically appropriate but, on reflection, quite as could be expected, if only we are intelligent and generous-minded enough to appreciate the relevant circumstances. In this sense we might say that Tolstoy's explanatory comments, like the apothegms of the great eighteenth-century French moralists from whom he had learnt so much, were essentially the fruits of common sense – widened, to be sure, and sharpened and sensitised to a quite uncommon degree. By contrast we shall find, when we pass to his full-length discussions of the intelligibility or unintelligibility of war and indeed of all history, that both the modesty and the effectiveness of his casual explanatory comments are lost: the intellectual aim becomes inappropriately inflated, and the illumination sadly diminished.

And, secondly, a few words about the range of application of Tolstoy's explanatory comments. Comparable comments in other eighteenth- and nineteenth-century novelists are concerned with individuals – with crucial moments, turns, revelations in their emotional lives and in the development of their character – or with small sets of matching individuals – rivals or lovers, or different pairs of rivals or lovers, or parents *vis-à-vis* their children for example. But in these latter instances, the explanatory comment usually works by moving rapidly – as does the dialogue or description of action – from one character to another, so that we understand what happens to the group through the successive or simultaneous moves and tensions, passions and interests of its different members, as illuminated or evidenced by the explanatory comment. And of course this is true of many passages and scenes in *War and Peace*. But Tolstoy's most characteristic and effective explanatory comments operate in a quite different way. They succeed in enlightening and explaining the *shared* feelings and attitudes and reactions of all members of a group, and in convincing us that such a group is capable, in appropriate circumstances, of achieving an astonishing degree of unspoken, unanalysed agreement and effective mutual adjustment. When, for example, the tragically divided Bolkonsky family, conversing about Pierre after his visit, find that they have nothing but good to say about him; or when the younger members of the Rostov family take up a line about some individual or some particular way of behaving, we are immediately convinced, by a few words of explanatory comment, not only that such unity of their attitudes is entirely true to life but is something of pre-eminent value in all social and family life. But even more powerful examples of this kind are to be found in Tolstoy's accounts of military life and action. To take only one example – the gallant resistance put up by the artillery captain Tushin and his team at the battle of Schön Graben. Tolstoy's comments on this action come close to being understatements; but, subtly interwoven with the narrative and dialogue, they help us to understand how heroic actions of this sort are performed in battle by the most ordinary – indeed often by the most unlikely-looking men. He remarks, for instance, that Tushin and his men initiated their inspired action and sustained it during hours of unceasing din, turmoil and horror, in a condition of feverish excitement, akin to delirium;[1] so that, when eventually forced to retreat, Tushin could as little understand why he was reprimanded by an officious staff officer as why he was picked out for signal gallantry by Prince Andrei. In this, as in countless other incidents in *War and Peace*, Tolstoy conveys to us what was for him the primary truth of war: namely that in war the most intelligible units of action are relatively small groups of men, in close physical contact and operationally interdependent, who share, as if by animal magnetism, the same reactions and feelings, whether in the form of resolution or faint-heartedness, of renewed dedication to, or of blind flight from, the demands of their terrible trade.

It is only in contrast to this primary truth (I suggest) that we can understand Tolstoy's detestation of, and complete rejection of, all high-falutin' theories of grand strategy and of the military genius of commanders who ride – and allegedly direct and control – the storms of battle. And, at the same time, this primary truth gives the lie to a view to which, in some of his anti-war polemics, Tolstoy appears to subscribe: namely that war *at all levels* is nothing but a confused and sordid mess, entirely lacking in intelligently co-ordinated direction of any kind. He lent particular support to this view when in 1901 he told a M. Paul Boyer that he had learnt everything he knew about war from Stendhal's description of the battle of Waterloo in chapter 3 of *La Chartreuse de Parme*, adding that he himself had verified Stendhal's claim that every great battle is a meaningless and undirected chaos, during his own military service in the Crimean War.[2] It is important to distinguish what is suggestive and interesting from what is evidently exaggerated and foolish in this claim on Tolstoy's part. In the first place, we must emphasise, Stendhal's account consists entirely in recalling the experiences – especially the bewilderment – of *one* participant in a battle, a participant incidentally who had no proper task to perform in it, since he (the young Fabrizio) is an Italian boy, who had only just arrived on the scene, having come of his own volition to fight for his hero 'the Emperor', and whose French is so imperfect that he lapses into Italian when questioned about his presence on the battlefield. Now one could easily agree that to so ill-equipped a participant in a battle – Tolstoy's Pierre on the field of Borodino was such another – everything he sees must seem totally inconsequential and unmeaning. But this is not to say that everything on a battlefield is in fact inconsequential and without meaning, or must seem to be so to all who take part in it. On the contrary, as Tolstoy himself shows us through numerous incidents, many of these understand perfectly well the job they have been set to do, even if the wider issues and ultimate justification (if any) of the battle or the war remain unknown to them.

So much, then, for what we may call the experienced truth of war, something that can be known to, or through the description of, only relatively small groups of men who share a common experience; and so much for the literary skill whereby Tolstoy recreates that experienced truth and persuades us to accept his accounts of it – the vividness of his descriptions compelling us to imagine that things were so, and the aptness of his comments convincing us that they must have been so, so that his finest passages read like self-verifying excerpts from a total record of war such as only God could know. But now we must remember that even if a battle or a campaign be an aggregation of the kinds of action, the experienced truth of which Tolstoy conveys to us, the process and logic of their aggregation is something that could not possibly be conveyed by any succession of descriptive sketches, no matter how detailed and vivid, no matter how convincingly confirmed by their accompanying explanatory comments. The structure of a battle as a whole is, by definition, something that could not be conveyed by Tolstoy's novelistic skill, since no one could conceivably *experience* a battle as a whole; and the kind of comment which is appropriate to descriptions of small group actions would be entirely out of place if applied to the vast, anonymous concatenations of men and material which make up a modern battle. Up to a point Tolstoy was aware of this; and it is part of his artistry that he frequently suggests the influence of vast, far-reaching events and aggregations of events – movements of men and nations and groups of nations – upon the small groups of individual soldiers that are the main and natural focus of his narratives. But it is notable that these references to background forces and influences are most effective when they are cast in very general and impressionistic terms, with no pretence of describing or explaining their mode of operation. On the other hand, however, from the beginning of Book 3 of *War and Peace* the element of explanatory comment, hitherto always tightly attached to particular incidents, begins to break loose from the novelistic narrative; and in the philosophical interludes which bulk larger as Books 3 and 4 proceed, it is quite evident that Tolstoy is trying to tell us something – perhaps a number of things – about battles and war regarded as wholes, which he believes to be of paramount importance.

What does Tolstoy's teaching at this larger, more general level amount to? On its positive side it strikes me as weak, almost trivial and half-hearted, quite out of keeping with his true intellectual character. On its negative or critical side, however, it contains a number of original ideas and arguments. Even if these are not used to the best advantage, even if we cannot accept the conclusion which Tolstoy derives from them, they deserve careful attention. For, although ostensibly worked out with the question of the *intelligibility* of wars and battles in mind, they in fact point forward to still larger questions – as to the necessity and the justifiability of wars – which supply the driving force of Tolstoy's best speculations and self-searchings in our area. But neither his positive nor his negative and critical teachings are at all adequately presented. (Philosophy by means of interludes in fictional and historical narrative is almost – but not quite – as useless as philosophy by contextless apothegms.) In order to assess what Tolstoy has to say, both positively and negatively, about wars and battles considered as wholes, we must first reflect for a moment on what I will risk calling the commonsense view of the relation between those individual and local actions which disclose the *experienced* truth of war and those vast clashes of armies which, chiefly for their political results, are commonly taken to contain the most *important*, if least easily agreed, truths of war. (Not, of course, that common sense has a clearly articulated view on this question. Here, as elsewhere in life, common sense is characterised by a sane but lazy disregard of difficult, even if very important, questions which it leaves to those whom it considers tiresomely clever and rather silly people, until the day comes when men must either face their difficult questions or perish.)

The sane but lazy position may often carry with it real temporary advantage, however. In the present instance it enables common sense to accept that the unity of an army in action – of a battle or a war – can have a great many different facets, whose interrelations may well defy explanation and even description, so that no general account of it can ever be entirely accurate or adequate. But, common sense insists, we all manage, nevertheless, to think of a battle or a war by means of a list of factors or facets which none of us would ever dream of denying, and which collectively keep the idea of its unity effectively if somewhat hazily before our minds. Among such factors are the following. Soldiers of any army have been recruited or press-ganged to fight for *one* cause, country or leader. Soldiers, while trained to their particular tasks, are also trained to give and to expect *support*, not indeed from their army as a whole, but from the units in immediate contact with them; and similarly, and over a wider field, with commanders at all levels as we ascend the ladder of command: performance of one's own task involves some appreciation of the wider tasks of the regiment, brigade, or division one belongs to. Still more positively, among senior officers, there is usually some appreciation of the overall plan of the battle or campaign which is expected or has actually begun. And finally there is the supreme commander's persistent application of, and adjustment of, his plan, as the campaign or battle proceeds. All these factors contribute to the unity – the strangely diffused, certainly not directly experienced or perceptible – unity of a war or battle considered as a whole, a unity which no one seriously questions, even if no one can claim to grasp or follow it with complete confidence and clarity.

But if this is the strength of the commonsense view, its weaknesses are no less plain. It suggests that *somehow* all the above factors, no doubt along with countless others, contribute to the effective unity of a battle or a war; but it says nothing of how they may or must affect one another, about which of them are logically or causally prior and which are subordinate, and so on. It suggests a table of contents or list of headings for the understanding of wars, but no instructions for identifying, let alone for resolving, war's most puzzling and problematic features. In truth, one could say that it is a view which works only so long as we do not find anything in the courses, processes and results of a war that *is genuinely problematic* – that is, so long as we accept the idea of the unity of a war or a battle quite unthinkingly, and do not raise any serious questions about the range of ways in which it can be expected to develop.

Tolstoy's discussions of wars or battles considered as wholes, fall into two groups, whose logical relations are not as simple as he supposes. On the one side we have his account of what a genuinely scientific understanding of any war would be. On the other side we have his tireless polemics against all applications, in the field of warfare, of the 'great men theory of history'. But in fact both the position which he commends (rather than provides) and the position which he deplores (and pulverises) have one very important feature in common. Both rest on a radical dissatisfaction with what I have called the commonsense view of the relation between the experienced truth, and the aggregate and more lasting truth of war. Tolstoy fails to notice this point, and because of this is unfairly biased against the 'great man theory' from the outset. But here another complication arises. While his discussion of what a genuinely scientific account of any war, regarded as a whole, would be like is weak, meagre and half-hearted, his attacks on the 'great men theory' are pushed home with all the ardour of a mind that knows it is on the scent of something really important. In fact all Tolstoy's original thoughts and feelings, puzzlement and concern, about the role of war in history – including the question of its indispensability or inexcusability – are much more powerfully expressed in his ostensibly negative polemics than in his ostensibly positive account of what a genuine, because scientific, understanding of war would amount to.

Let us see, first, what he tells us on the latter score. A truly scientific understanding of any large-scale military engagement, Tolstoy insists, would require a total transformation of the commonsense view, in respect of terminology, interest, presupposition and expectations. Instead of regarding war as a somewhat loose form of purposive, rationally directed activity, we should have to think of it as a phase in the unplanned movements, convergences and clashes of human societies, operating in accordance with the as yet undiscovered laws of 'social dynamics'. Nations or groups of nations in interaction will never be understood, he continues, until their moves are analysed down to what he calls the 'human differential'[3] and are represented as being in continuous motion by methods akin to Newtonian calculus. Evidently what he has in mind is a version of what has since come to be known as the 'physicalist' programme for the explanation of human behaviour. No doubt Tolstoy's acute sense of the infectiousness of feeling and reaction in small groups of men in the face of horrifying danger, offers a clue to what he meant by the 'human differential' – a possible unit of socially significant changes of bodily motion and feeling. But he no-where offers us even a sketch of how his imagined 'social dynamics' would work, of what he supposes its principal variables must be or of the nature of the determining relations between them. This is why one cannot but regard this part of his thought as both pretentious and trivial. And it is worth noting that Tolstoy never returned to, never tried to develop, his idea of a Newton-like explanation of human con-duct, in any of his later writings. Indeed, I think one could go farther and say that Tolstoy's attempts to sketch a scientific approach to the understanding of war was nothing but a very ill-chosen way of ex-pressing a much more important truth which, although in outwardly very different forms, dominates his thought about war from *War and Peace* to the pacifist essays of his old age. This is that because so much in the process and results of any battle or war must *in fact* remain obscure and inexplicable, the really serious questions about war – about its uses and excuses, its avoidability or inescapability, its justification or utter unjustifiability – do not call for any great cleverness or expertise. On the contrary, in an area where so much must remain obscure, dark, unanalysable and unappraisable, the only possible answers have to be extremely simple. But before we come to this critical moment in Tolstoy's thought, we must first look at the main lines of his attack upon his *bête noir*, the 'great men theory of history'.

According to Tolstoy, all military historians have dealt with the problem we have been discussing in much the same way. Instead of seeking to transform totally the commonsense explanation of how one army acts as a whole against another, they have reduced the never-ending list of factors that might be relevant to the action to one crucial factor which, they claim, alone makes possible an understanding of what actually happens in a battle or campaign. What is this key factor? It is the plan in accordance with which the successful, dominant, victorious commander organises, directs and operates all the forces at his disposal in the light of all the various factors and circumstances which common sense points to in explanation of an army's unity-in-action. It is only in the light of that plan – the expression of the victorious commander's insight and will – that we can find meaning, structure, intelligibility in what otherwise must seem, as Stendhal and others have maintained, a chaos of meaningless slaughter, flight and terror. Or, to put the same point in another way, the total action of an army is not only, in the nature of things, something that could not conceivably be experienced, perceived, empathised with: it is the sort of action that could not conceivably *occur* except in accordance with the firm and comprehensive orders of a single directing mind. Sometimes historians are in a position to know exactly what these orders were; and then we are in a position to understand what happens – indeed we can sometimes do so even when the plan breaks down. At other times, however, we have to infer what the victorious commander's orders must have been from what we know to have happened. In either case, however, it is the victorious commander's plan and orders that are decisive, from the point of view of historical understanding as much as from that of the military result. And we have a well-known extension of this truth in the fairly familiar situation, well exemplified in Napoleon's career, in which the fame and fear of an all-conquering general virtually paralyses his adversaries' will, since they are convinced from the outset that his plans must be superior to their own.

Such in outline is the 'great men theory' as applied to military history; and in the second epilogue of *War and Peace*, as well as in the numerous philosophical passages in Books 3 and 4, Tolstoy assails this theory from a number of different angles. His first argument is an application of the general determinist thesis which he assumed, like most of his nineteenth-century contemporaries, that all science and therefore all genuine understanding requires.[4] All historical evidence suggests that the decisions of great men – kings, potentates, supreme commanders, etc. are determined in much the same ways as the decisions of other men – their motives, as all those close to them have averred, are in the main as petty, as one-sided, as egoistic, as much swayed by the considerations of the moment, as those of the rest of us. Therefore the suggestion that they have a special capacity which enables them to direct and co-ordinate in wholly intelligible fashion the movements of hundreds and thousands of men – of whose actual condition and position they are inevitably ignorant – is absurd. The organisation, coherence, order and intelligibility of vast armies cannot therefore be understood in terms of the peculiarly competent judgments and decisions and orders of a few men of extraordinary intelligence, occupying positions of extraordinary power. This is not a very strong argument, although it can be used to score points off the 'great men theory'. It neglects the fact that military commanders have access to much more information – however imperfect much of it may be – and have also the benefit of much more professional advice than others, e.g. junior commanders, common soldiers, who are involved in a battle. It also neglects, to an absurd extent, the importance of training and experience in the direction of military operations and two more general capacities which are essential to success in almost every branch of public life – that of delegating and yet still appearing to be in complete command, and that of using one's position to inspire confidence in the rightness of one's decisions. (Tolstoy, incidentally, gives us a splendid example of both these capacities in his portrayal of Bagration, in the battle of Schön Graben).[5] But further, Tolstoy fails to notice that the decisions required of a military commander – or, for that matter, of the organisers, of any large-scale undertaking – *are* often of a very different character from those demanded of the rest of us in even the severest crises of public or personal life. A commander-in-chief's decisions are often of what might be called an algebraic kind: he has to try to keep in mind and take into account factors of *any* sort that might affect *any* of the units under his command. Such decisions do not call (as Napoleon once claimed) for something like mathematical genius: but rather for an extension of what is vulgarly called horse sense, or all-round awareness of one's situation, in the most distracting and unnerving of circumstances. Now it is a simple fact of life that some otherwise very ordinary men have a capacity for such decision-making in a very high degree; and this gives some support to the 'great men theory' even if it is unacceptable on other grounds.

Tolstoy's second argument against the 'great men theory' is even weaker, and depends upon 'guying' that theory to a point where it becomes so absurd as hardly to merit refutation.[6] If it is maintained that the will of one man is sufficient to set in motion, to keep in motion, and to change the direction and rate of motion, of a vast army – or equally well the arrangements of a nation or of a vast commercial concern – then, Tolstoy argues, ordinary commonsense reflection can assure us that such a claim is absurd. For it is obvious that the failure of any number of humble individuals in their particular duties, or the failure of any number of parts or connections of the machinery or organisation which they make use of, can be sufficient to frustrate and render useless the ablest imaginable judgements and the clearest imaginable orders as to how the desired end shall be brought about: no matter what genius such judgements or orders may display, if the wheels stick, so do they. But a much more plausible and natural form of the 'great men theory' would be as follows: at many stages of a campaign or a battle, a decision taken by a senior, and in particular by a supreme commander, is likely to produce far more extensive and crucial changes in the over-all progress and eventual result of the engagement, than any decision on the part of a junior commander or private soldier could be expected to do. Tolstoy's second criticism, in fact, is little more than a heavy-handed correction of the well-known habit of historians who speak of General A's attack, General B's counter-thrust, General C's stubborn defence, etc., as if the respective generals *were* their armies, or were indeed responsible for their armies' every action, perhaps even for their recruitment, training and equipment. But to accuse even the stupidest of military historians of thinking like this is itself the height of absurdity.

Tolstoy's third argument is of much greater interest, although again it fails to demolish the 'great men theory'. He argues that no com-mander could ever exert a decisive overall influence upon a campaign or battle because 'he never finds himself at the beginning of an event'[7] – the position from which, Tolstoy maintains, historians and amateur strategists invariably tend to imagine things. In fact, however, 'the general is always in the midst of a series of shifting events and so can never at any point deliberate upon the whole impact of what is going on'. This, we may recall, comes very close to Clausewitz's account of the difficulties with which every general has to cope in coming to his decisions in the heat and confusion of battle. What Tolstoy's point proves, however, is not that generals, 'in the midst of a series of shifting events' cannot really decide anything, but only that even their most strenuous and difficult decisions remain subject to modifications while the battle lasts. Military decision is always a matter of constant im-provisation and constant adaption and readaption of plans to meet rapidly changing dangers and opportunities. But of course this is not to say that the decisions of military commanders are necessarily otiose or ineffective.

Tolstoy's fourth and final argument is of even greater interest. He begins by pointing out that no military commander ever, strictly speaking, *orders* such a vast operation as, say, the conquest of Russia or the invasion of England; although it is chiefly in connection with such vast designs that military genius is commonly acclaimed.[8] Vague, rhetorical pronouncements and promises may be made on such a sub-ject; but actual military orders always relate to specified, tangible objectives, and have to be accompanied by detailed instructions as to the ways and means of reaching those objectives. But secondly such orders almost inevitably meet with unforeseen difficulties, in view of which they have to be continually reiterated or revised or replaced *in toto*. The consequence is that every military operation of any complexity proceeds to a *succession* of orders, all of which, after the initial ones, are greatly influenced by the reaction of the enemy and the changes in the position and general condition of one's own forces. An even more important consequence for our present discussion is that of all the orders that are given for a particular campaign or battle, only a comparatively small number – namely those that are actually suited to the situation – are in fact carried out. The others, those from which no effective action could possibly issue, are usually forgotten – since they have to be quickly replaced by orders of a more appropriate kind. From this Tolstoy deduces that, in actual war, an order is *never* the cause of the event which follows. 'Our erroneous idea' he writes, 'that the command which *precedes* the event *causes* the event is due to the fact that when the event has taken place and out of thousands of commands those few which were consistent with the event have been executed [realised], we forget about the others that were not executed because they could not be' (my italics throughout).[9] The fallacy, which Tolstoy here claims to have exposed, is that of *post hoc, ergo propter hoc*. But he also claims that this fallacy is compounded by another: namely that because the results of a military event are often considered as a single whole, e.g. as a victory or as a surrender, we are naturally inclined to consider the succession of commands that preceded it as likewise forming a single whole, i.e. a single master-plan, or single act of will of some great commander. This is a strong argument against the age-old fallacy of unjustified reification, to which historians of war are particularly prone.

The positive direction in which this argument leads us is clearly shown in one of its later formulations. Tolstoy writes, with his majestic gift for simplification, 'Men are hauling a log. Each of them may be expressing an opinion as to how and where it should be hauled. They haul the log to its destination, and it turns out that it has been done in accordance with what one of them said. *He gave the command*' (my italics).[10] It is obvious that the purpose of this passage is to deflate, virtually to zero, the significance of commands in all social or collective activity, and especially in war. Tolstoy does this by suggesting that the speech functions of indicating, suggesting, or persuading are indistinguishable in certain situations from the speech function of commanding. The suggestion is intelligent, and many features of speech in urgent action situations confirm it. But the argument nevertheless rests on a number of untenable assumptions. It assumes, first, that the act of hauling can somehow have a destination without someone's commanding or suggesting it and most of the haulers agreeing to it. It assumes, further, that the coincidence between what someone said (or suggested) and the *destination actually achieved* is, in all such cases, logically contingent – almost as if someone had been singing Tipperary and the log happened to end up right there. But however slight and tenuous the effect of orders on a battle, they are not accidental in that sense or to that degree. Finally, it assumes that what actually happens in a battle is always one of a number of possibilities which *could* have been envisaged by an intelligent and informed participant, quite irrespective of the commands that were actually given and actually obeyed. Such and such moves were serious possibilities. Others were not. But the very fact that a quite unexpected command *is* given, and begins to be executed, may alter the whole face of a battle – the whole range of possibilities which it presents. What previously seemed impossible, or to offer too slight a chance of success to be seriously considered, may suddenly be seen to be of the first importance. (Or as Napoleon is reported to have said, 'Engage the enemy and see what happens.') From this point of view, we may conclude that a commander's orders, while certainly not possessing any all-conquering magic, may sometimes turn out to have been more than practically decisive: they may have revealed *facts* – what was actually there, what was actually happening – which otherwise might have remained altogether unknown.

In these last arguments Tolstoy shows himself a most penetrating critic of military history, military legend, and military thinking in general. Yet, even when one must admire him most, one cannot but be worried by the almost frenzied fanaticism with which he attacks the 'great men theory of history', especially as applied to warfare. How is this intellectual violence to be explained? Partly, no doubt, by a certain lack of personal balance. (So long as he narrates Tolstoy's balance is flawless: as soon as he begins to philosophise it becomes uncertain). But much more important, in my opinion, are the following considerations which I now wish to pursue. First, in almost all his philosophising about war, what he has chiefly in mind is one campaign: the French invasion of, and ruinous retreat from, Russia in 1812–13. This was, no doubt, the greatest event in the greatest European war before our century. But, judged by the standards of its time, it was one of the strangest, least typical, of campaigns known to history. Secondly, Tolstoy's diatribes against the 'great men theory' are most devastatingly exemplified in his characterisation of Napoleon, both as an individual human being and as a national and military legend. For Tolstoy, the Napoleonic legend embodies in its most loathsomely intoxicating form the lie of war; it is the real villain of his story, whom, as we might say reversing his dictum in *Sebastopol*, he loathes with all the energy of his soul. But thirdly, the lie of war penetrates all – or all but the purest and strongest – of those who come in contact with it. The highest professionals, the military experts, either lie about it or else rave about it in their bouts of self-assertion – as Prince Andrei discovers, listening to the zany discussion of what the Russians should do with their strongly armed position on the Drissa. The young self-pushers, the Borises and the Bergs, even the good-natured Nikolai, lie about their exploits in war, either out of calculated policy or driven by some unaccountable compulsion. The drawing-room strategists talk with nauseatingly false knowledgeability about war's higher principles; young society girls indulge in absurd daydreams of what their heroic lovers are doing – doing for *their* sakes of course; while mature men, nobles and merchants, are carried away on waves of wartime hysteria, which they do not stop to question, until they remember what they have committed themselves to pay towards keeping the war in motion.

But in all this falsity, the myth of the great heroic commander of genius stands head and shoulders above all other lies; and it is therefore worth recalling in outline how Tolstoy's witch-hunt of Napoleon develops in the course of *War and Peace*. In Book 1, in which the narrative culminates in the Battle of Austerlitz, the character of Napoleon is left undiscussed, although there are hints about it, as deft as they are just, in the scene where Napoleon rides through the swathes of dead and wounded after the battle. But the unfolding of the narrative suggests that, in comparison with his Russian and Austrian opposite numbers, Napoleon did possess a military flair that could very naturally be taken for genius. And Tolstoy ascribes to Prince Andrei an attitude to Napoleon which must have been common to many of the ablest military men of the age: an admiration for his prowess and daring which came close to hero-worship, combined with a determination to cut him down to size in his role of national enemy. But from the opening of Book 3, which describes the fateful crossing of the Niemen in June 1812, Napoleon is presented, alternately, as something close to a criminal lunatic – a violent and unbridled megalomaniac dicing with hundreds and thousands of lives – and, on other pages, as a pitiable creature of circumstances or tool of fate, who deludedly believes he is commanding an operation of incomparable importance and complexity, but who in fact (or so Tolstoy maintains) is achieving less through all he imagines he is doing, than the lowliest of the soldiers under his command. When in this mood, Tolstoy treats Napoleon as an object of pity – but of pity which inevitably passes into disgust. Considered as a man, Napoleon is subject to many changes of mood; in some of them we may feel with him, in others we may hate or despise him. But as a legend, as the embodiment of all the falsity of his own legend, he is presented as wholly evil. In this respect he is, in Tolstoy's belief, at one with all other allegedly great commanders, who are the shameless front men or deluded mascots of titanic forces which they have never even begun to understand, yet are worshipped as the guides and guardians of the destinies of their nations.

This suggests that most wars, and in particular great wars, have been wholly misunderstood by even the most intelligent of those who have taken part in them. And if this is so it must follow that questions of the use, the necessity, and still more the justification of wars have never been properly posed, still less satisfactorily answered. How, and to what extent, does Tolstoy try to answer them in *War and Peace*? In view of his obsessive concern with the 'truth of war', it is surely an astonishing fact that, in all the philosophical passages of *War and Peace*, the question of, in particular, the justification of war is hardly raised at all. Why is this? One reason is that the strictly determinist – almost 'physicalist' – standpoint from which these philosophical passages are written make it difficult to formulate and apply strong and searching moral judgments and distinctions. When all parties are seen as pawns in a game, whose main moves and dominant forces are as yet incomprehensible, praise and blame, commendation and condemnation, are unlikely to be applied confidently and illuminatingly. A second reason is this. War has usually been condemned by moralists for combining a number of general human vices in a particularly intense and horrifying way. But suppose one took the view, as Tolstoy did like Kant before him, that war is at once the supreme exemplar and the main source of all human wickedness; then any condemnation of it or any explanation of its necessity, resting on more general grounds, would evidently be otiose. All that one could do would be to point to particular instances of the evil of war, and let these speak for themselves, so clearly and indeed so shockingly, that no further comment or explanation is possible. And this is, in effect, what Tolstoy does. It is one of the greatest proofs of his artistic wisdom that he presents his condemnation of war, and his account of the only conditions under which men are justified in resorting to it, not in a laboured philosophical digression, but in one of the most movingly and tragically terrifying scenes in the whole of *War and Peace*.

On the eve of Borodino, Pierre who has 'come to see the battle' – although in a very different spirit from that which brought young Fabrizio to Waterloo – asks to be taken to the quarter of his friend Prince Andrei, who will be mortally wounded in the battle on the following day. Shortly after they arrive, two German staff officers in the Russian service ride past, and Prince Andrei recognises them as Wolzogen and Clausewitz.

'The war must be extended over a wider area. This is a conviction which I cannot advocate too highly,' one of them was saying.

'Oh undoubtedly', replied the other, 'since the aim is to wear out the enemy, one cannot, of course, take into account damage and injury suffered by private persons.'

'Oh yes, spread the war!', said Prince Andrei with an angry snort, when they had ridden by. 'In that "wider area" I had a father and son and a sister at Bald Hills [his family home]. He doesn't care about that. That's what I was just saying to you – those German gentlemen won't win the battle tomorrow, they will only make a mess of it. . .they have nothing in their German heads but theories not worth an empty egg-shell, while their hearts are void of the one thing that's needed for tomorrow, which Timohin [his simple, trusty second-in-command] has.'. . .But in a few moments Prince Andrei's feverish anger turned upon the French. 'One thing I would do if I had the power. I would not take prisoners. . .Not to take prisoners! That by itself would transform the whole aspect of war and make it less cruel. . .They prate about the rules of warfare, of chivalry, of flags of truce and humanity to the wounded. . .All fiddle-sticks. I saw chivalry and flags of truce in 1805: they humbugged us and we humbugged them. They plunder people's homes,. . .kill our children and our fathers, and then talk of the rules of warfare and generosity to a fallen foe. No quarter, *I* say, but kill and be killed! Anyone who has reached this conclusion through the same suffering as I have. . .'

He was unexpectedly pulled up in his argument by a cramp in his throat. He walked to and fro a few times in silence. . .he began to speak again.

'If there was none of this magnanimity business in warfare, *we should never go to war, except for something worth facing certain death for, as now*. . .[And then] it would be war! And then the spirit and determination of the fighting men would be something quite different. All these Westphalians and Hessians that Napoleon has dragged at his heels would never have come to Russia, and we should not have gone fighting in Austria and

Prussia without knowing why. War is not a polite recreation, but the vilest thing in life, and we ought to understand that and not play at war. Our attitude towards *the fearful necessity of war ought to be stern and serious*. It boils down to this: we should have done with humbug, and let war be war and not a game.' [My italics throughout][11]

For Prince Andrei, then, and we may presume for Tolstoy also at this stage of his thought, men 'should never go to war except for something worth facing certain death for, as now'. Dramatically convincing as this conclusion is in its context – with Prince Andrei speaking as a man who foresees and almost wills his own death, and with neither Pierre nor any of those present having any answer to his terrifying outburst – yet its practical message is by no means as clear as one could wish. If construed literally, the claim that war is justified only for men who recognise that, by fighting, they will certainly be killed, must in many cases be a practical contradiction. Self-sacrifice, even certain self-immolation, is sometimes required of men: but only with a view to destroying or lessening some intolerable evil. Without this hope and aim, which may often be of the slenderest or achievable only by the most indirect and uncertain means, self-sacrifice would be a pointless self-removal from evil rather than even a forlorn protest against it. Yet it takes only a moment's reflection to recognise that to fight an evil, but only on the condition that one will be killed in fighting it, is in most cases to weaken immeasurably one's chances of destroying the evil in question. If, on the other hand, one construes Prince Andrei's position less literally, as meaning that the only justifiable wars are those in which men know that there are no alternatives, no mean results, between victory and certain death, then its moral persuasiveness is immediately lost. Countless brave men have gone into battle, accepting this all-or-nothing choice, but for the very worst of causes, so that their self-sacrifice becomes indistinguishable from an atavistic madness. How, then, is Prince Andrei's terrible speech to be interpreted?

The key to it lies in his claim that if, by a well-understood convention, war meant fighting to the death for either side – i.e. if there were to be no taking of prisoners, no flags of truce, etc. – then the Hessians and Westphalians would never have invaded Russia, nor Russian troops have invaded Prussia and Austria *without knowing why*. More generally, war can be justified only when it takes the form of an ultimate, extreme deterrent of those seemingly minor and tolerable wars which, in fact, always involve outrageous injustice and suffering on either side; or, to speak more paradoxically but more tellingly, only when it is *known* that war will take a form so terrible that the mere prospect of it suffices to inhibit all traditional inclinations or excuses for lapsing into war. Thus construed, Prince Andrei's thesis could be taken to anticipate recent theories of 'massive deterrence' – especially by the threat of nuclear attack – theories which have not proved either strategically feasible or morally tolerable in practice. It also shows a marked similarity to those defences of the death penalty for murder which admit its all-but-intolerable inhumanity, but which urge that this very aspect of it provides a necessary deterrent of even greater inhumanities on a much wider scale. And it will at once occur to readers of Tolstoy's later works that he came to reject the death penalty as vehemently as he rejected all resorts to war and justifications of war, no matter how terrible the circumstances or the probable consequences might be.

As against this, however, we should notice one important if negative continuity linking the justification of war which Tolstoy puts into the mouth of Prince Andrei with the absolute pacifism of his later years. Both positions rest on a rejection of the idea that traditional uses of force between political communities can in some way be rationalised, in the sense of being brought and kept within tolerable limits, through the exercise of Reason. As against the view to which, albeit in very different ways, so many other humane thinkers have subscribed, Tolstoy insists, at both stages of his thought, that violence – especially when organised by the state for both external purposes (war) and internal purposes (oppression) – has a momentum and also an insidious attraction of its own, against which Reason, anyhow as ordinarily conceived, is completely powerless. Any effective counter to war, or to militaristic oppression, called for other-than-rational sanctions – subrational, as when violence is magnified to the point where it becomes its own deterrent, or superrational as where Christian love meets and opposes it by altogether non-violent means. The former alternative, as expressed by Prince Andrei, marks the apogee of Tolstoy's struggle to reach the truth of war in *War and Peace*: the latter, perhaps the central pillar of the strangely ascetic, non-traditional, virtually non-theological Christianity of his old age, is expressed, if not with the same dramatic persuasiveness, at least with unforgettably savage satire, and occasional deep pathos and prophetic power, in *Christianity and Pacifism* and *The Kingdom of God is within You*.

These essays were written between 1892 and 1894, the years following Tolstoy's outstandingly successful relief and protest work in connection with the famine in the Tula and Samara districts of Russia. This work damaged Tolstoy's health, but it did his morale a world of good; and the essays breathe a self-confidence and assert an attractive natural authority which are often lacking in his later writings. It will be convenient to deal first with the later and shorter *Christianity and Pacifism*, because it is artistically much the more effective of the essays and provides the modern reader with a most attractive introduction to Tolstoy in the role of pacifist prophet.

It is essentially an attack on the Franco–Russian *accorde* of 1891, and on the allegedly spontaneous enthusiasm displayed by both nations for the military alliance which followed. Tolstoy tells us that the crudely contrived celebrations, and still more the reporting of them in the Russian and French newspapers, filled him first with amusement, then with perplexity, then with indignation; and he conveys these successive reactions with great literary skill. In his opening pages he makes free use of Russian newspaper reports of the reception given in Toulon to a Russian naval squadron from Kronstadt. The speeches of admirals, ministers, diplomats, bishops and others on that occasion reached a level of absurdity rare even in the annals of international jamborees. But Tolstoy's dead-pan descriptions and comments brilliantly suggest the precarious character of the whole affair, poised between crazy comedy and monstrous self-delusion. Here are a few excerpts:

The speeches generally ended as if with a refrain, with the words; 'Toulon–Kronstadt' or 'Kronstadt–Toulon'. And the names of those places where so many different dishes had been eaten and so many different wines had been drunk, were pronounced as words recalling the most noble and heroic actions of the representatives of both nations – words that left nothing more to be said since all was understood. We love one another and we love peace. Kronstadt–Toulon! What more could be added to that?. . .especially when said to the triumphal music of bands playing two hymns at the same time: the one hymn glorifying the Tsar and imploring God to send him all prosperity, the other cursing all tsars and kings and invoking destruction upon them.

And all these strange actions were accompanied by even stranger religious rites and public prayers to which one supposed the French had long become unaccustomed. So many public prayers as during that brief period had hardly been performed since the time of the Concordat. . .Thus a bishop at Toulon at the launching of the ironclad *Jorigiberi* prayed to the God of peace, letting it be felt however that in case of need he could also apply to the God of war. . .

Meanwhile tens of thousands of telegrams were flying from Russia to France and from France to Russia. French women greeted the Russian

women. Russian women expressed their gratitude to the French women. . .
Russian children wrote greetings in verse to French children, French
children replied in verse and in prose. The Russian Minister of Education
testified to the French Minister of Education of the sudden feelings of
love for the French entertained by all the teachers and writers under his
supervision. The Society for the Protection of Animals testified its ardent
attachment to the French, and a similar announcement was made by the
Municipality of Kazán. . .

To say nothing of the millions of working days wasted on these
festivities or the wholesale drunkenness (connived at by all the authorities)
of those who took part in them, to say nothing of the senselessness of the
speeches that were delivered, most insane and cruel things were done and
no one paid any attention to them.

Thus some dozens of people were crushed to death and no one found it
necessary to refer to it. A correspondent wrote that a Frenchman told him
at a ball that there was now hardly a woman in Paris who would
not betray her duty to satisfy the desire of any of the Russian sailors. And
all this passed unnoticed as though it ought to be so. There were even
cases of unmistakable insanity. One woman for instance put on a dress of
the colours of the French and Russian flags, and having waited for the
arrival of the sailors, cried: '*Vive la Russie!*' and jumped from the bridge
into the river and was drowned.[12]

From these bacchanalian scenes Tolstoy switches to a recent report,
in the Kiev University Records, of a psychical epidemic in a number of
villages in the province, to which the writer, a Professor of Psychiatry,
had given the name Malevanism. Under the influence of a religious
revivalist named Malevánov the villagers, like many others before
them, began to believe that the world would shortly come to an end,
and thereupon began to give away all their possessions, to dress themselves up, to become sentimentally disposed to one another, to be very
talkative, to shed facile tears of joy, to buy parasols and kerchiefs as
adornments, to visit one another – all ordinary work having been abandoned – to eat and give each other sweetmeats, and to repeat stereotyped
phrases like 'If I want to work, I work; if I don't want to, why should
I?' Tolstoy maintains that in this so-called psychopathic epidemic
(which the Professor strongly advised the government to prevent from
spreading) we find all the features of the Toulon–Kronstadt madness,
only in a much more innocent form. The poor Malevanists were in for
a rude awakening one fine morning, but the millions who were influenced by the Toulon–Kronstadt madness would wake up one morning
to a general European war. And as a first proof of this, Tolstoy points
out that, as with the bishop's speech at the launching of the iron-clad,
so in all the speeches of ministers and admirals the references to peace

are dragged in clumsily, irrelevantly, and often with an odious hypocrisy. The euphoria surrounding the Franco–Russian accounts demanded that there should be no mention of war, in particular no mention of a possible war with Germany, which nevertheless everyone knew to be the whole point of the alliance. This made the celebration not only absurd but bad: bad because it was an obvious and shameless lie, and a lie which would terminate in murder. There follows a passage of such penetrating, indeed agonising, accuracy that it must be quoted extensively.

The bells will peal and long-haired men will dress themselves in gold-embroidered sacks and begin to pray on behalf of murder. The familiar, age-old, horrible business will recommence. The editors of newspapers will set to work to arouse hatred and murder under the guise of patriotism and will be delighted to double their sales. Manufacturers, merchants, and contractors for army-stores, will hurry about joyfully in expectation of doubled profits. Officials of all sorts will busy themselves in the hope of being able to steal more than usual. Army commanders will bustle here and there, drawing double pay and rations and hoping to receive various trinkets, ribbons, crosses, stripes, and stars, for murdering people. Idle ladies and gentlemen will fuss about, entering their names in advance for the Red Cross and getting ready to bandage those whom their husbands and brothers are setting out to kill – imagining that they will be doing a most Christian work thereby.

And hundreds of thousands of simple kindly folk, torn from peaceful toil and from their wives, mothers, and children, and with murderous weapons in their hands, will trudge wherever they may be driven, stifling the despair in their souls by songs, debauchery, and vodka. They will march, freeze, suffer from hunger, and fall ill. Some will die of disease, and some will at last come to the place where men will kill them by the thousand. And they too, without themselves knowing why, will murder thousands of others whom they had never before seen, and who had neither done nor could do them any wrong.[13]

But not only, Tolstoy argues, were the celebrations in Toulon and Paris a lie because their motive was much less peace than war; the main emotion which they were intended to intensify, and in whose name the next war would be fought – namely patriotism – was very far from being the simple and central force in all nations which politicians and publicists assume it to be. On the contrary, Tolstoy claims – repeating an observation made by Turgenev nearly a half century earlier – that Russian peasants are almost completely devoid of patriotism, which is a phenomenon of the cities and for the most part an artificially whipped up, synthetic emotion. The myth of patriotism – of the unique value and innocence and peculiar vulnerability of one's own country in the face of evil forces – has been invented to sustain and increase the power of governments and of the classes which execute governmental orders in return for social and economic privileges. Without this myth, the bulk of the population of any country would never tolerate the burdens and horrors that are imposed upon it in both peace and war. From this point on, Tolstoy proceeds to summarise an argument which is much more fully developed in *The Kingdom of God is within you*. Once remove the myth of patriotism, which is an affront to the universality of Christian ethics, and the absurdity, as well as the wickedness, of all war-like plans and preparation will be made manifest. Different peoples will begin to recognise, without difficulty, how very like each other they all are, and to what an extent their preoccupations, anxieties and reasonable hopes of happiness are the same. Here Tolstoy rests his case on arguments which he takes over from the leading liberal and socialist prophets of his century, adding only one important note of his own. Although war is an evil necessity of *all* governments, constitutional as well as arbitrary, Tolstoy emphasises that the emotions surrounding war turn it into the most terrible of all human temptations. The great mass of men, as he repeats again and again, are *hypnotised* into war, by their governments in the first instance, but alas, and even more remarkably, by each other. But by nailing the lie of patriotism, we can begin to rescue men from their hypnotised condition, and to save them, not so much from each other, as from themselves.

This conclusion may seem facile, and sadly lacking in political substance and direction. But the essay was not intended as a fully argued defence of Christian Pacifism, or as a guide to action in any particular situation. It is literature used as an offensive, or at least as a provocative weapon: a bombshell tossed into what is commonly taken to be the moral stronghold of militarism, with a view to waking people up, and shaking the easy assumption that there can be no harm in international get-togethers, however foolish the forms they take. And thus understood, it is a masterpiece of political propaganda.

*The Kingdom of God is within you* is a much longer, more searching, more self-revealing, but a much less readable, less artistically unified, sustained and directed piece of work. Some of its finest paragraphs show an intellectual strength and daring, and others a prophetic simplicity and pathos, which are unique in Tolstoy's writings; but equally, although a serious work of exploration, in which Tolstoy tries to make clear to himself as much as to his readers the implications of his new-found political vision, it betrays the limitations of that vision, and indeed of Tolstoy's capacity for sustained political thought. Its opening chapters deal in a rather perfunctory way with the undeniable anarcho-pacifist strand in Christianity from its earliest days, with the striking consistency with which that strand has been either neglected or denied by all established or state-captured churches, and with its recent revival among a number of English, American, German and Slavonic sects. Tolstoy then widens his canvas, and in two remarkable chapters, entitled 'Lack of understanding of Christianity by believers' and 'Misconceptions of Christianity by Men of Science' says almost everything that needed to be said about the patent spiritual poverty both of most Christian churches and most of their 'rationalist' opponents in nineteenth-century Europe. Christianity, he goes on to tell us, consists in a radically new pattern of life inspired by a new idea of human fulfilment. In this respect it replaces both what he calls, rather ineptly, the personal or animal conception of life which prompts men to live for their individual, instinctive satisfactions, and the social or pagan conception of life, which encourages men to find their satisfaction as members of some particular group or aggregate in opposition to other groups or aggregates. All dominant nineteenth-century doctrines, including positivism and communism, are social and pagan in the sense just defined; they promise fulfilment to the individual by uniting him to an actual aggregate or totality of individuals. Christianity, by contrast, unites him to the origin of all life, which is love or God; and the pattern of life demanded by this unity is clearly spelt out, Tolstoy claims, in the Sermon on the Mount.

He next tries to develop this idea of Christianity as a way of life, in a manner which has many parallels in nineteenth-century thought – most notably in the later thoughts of Kant and some of the earlier thoughts of Marx, although it is quite certain that Tolstoy had read none of their relevant writings. He urges that, while the Christian pattern of life was clearly formulated nearly two millennia ago – and had been adumbrated in various ways long before that – it is only in the modern world, because of greater density of population, increased intercourse between nations, a greater mastery of nature and the accumulation of knowledge, that the immediate economic and social conditions of life make it, not only morally obligatory, but practically feasible and indeed practically indispensable, if the most terrible disasters are to be avoided. The thoughts – or rather many of the now unthinking assumptions – of most European men have been Christianised to a considerable extent, Tolstoy believes; but the transition to a practical Christianity, or a way of life in accordance with the Sermon on the Mount, will be by no means easy. A combination of factors – notably social inertia, the temptations of privilege, and the belief that force is as essential to peace at home as to war abroad – are arrayed against it. This unholy alliance is the real theme, providing the hatred that is the real inspiration, of the book which carries so misleadingly quietistic a title.

On the face of it *The Kingdom of God is within you* is a systematic, if heretically grounded, exposition of the Christian Pacifist case against war. But anyone who reads it in this sense is likely to be disappointed, and is certain to miss the best things that it contains. In the first place, and with no disrespect to his intense spiritual struggles and acute moral perceptions, it may be doubted whether Tolstoy can properly be called a Christian, since he adhered to none of the distinctive tenets of any known Christian church. Consider, for instance, the following affirmation from the closing paragraphs of *The Kingdom of God is within you*: 'No external efforts can safeguard our life which is inevitably attended by unavoidable suffering and ends in yet more inevitable death. . .our life can have no other meaning than the constant fulfilment of what is demanded of us by the Power that has. . . given us. . .our rational consciousness.'[14] This expresses a noble attitude which is by no means unique to Tolstoy; it comes very close to that which inspired Immanuel Kant. But of Christian theology, Christian eschatology, Christian hope and humility, or of special devotion to the figure of Christ, it contains not a trace. What Tolstoy *called* Christianity was an all-consuming passion to make sense of life and death as known in this world, and more particularly to find a morally tolerable response to what seemed to him the central political fact of his time: namely that whereas what he called the Christian conception of life was due to replace the social or pagan conception, this progress was being resisted, with hideously corrupting consequences, by the dominance, in Russia and to some degree in all modern states, of militaristic interests and habits of thought. Moreover Tolstoy was quite as much concerned with the political – in the sense of domestic and bureaucratic – manipulations of militarism as with its more obvious expression in war. Indeed, the employment and continuous build-up of centrally controlled armed forces to preserve the existing social order, in all European countries but most especially in backward Russia, seemed to him to have been the main cause of the ever-intensifying wars of modern Europe. Again, we should notice that while war seemed to Tolstoy to be the apogee of the wickedness of the modern world – masses of men of different nations being driven to slay each other to preserve the privilege of their respective oppressors – it was not the sheer act of killing that most horrified him. The act of killing was indeed for him a terrible thing; but when committed by a border-thief like Hadji Murad, the hero of his last and in some ways most wonderful story, or by a young conscript ordered to fire, it was understandable and forgiveable. What could not be forgiven, what could not be excused, was the progressive domination of life by the anonymous, irresistible, seemingly irreversible-bureaucratic state machines. Tolstoy writes best about these in *The Kingdom of God is within you* where he writes most simply, as in the following sentences:

The most cruel and terrible band of robbers is not so much to be dreaded as such a State organization. The authority of a robber chief is to a certain degree limited by members of his band who retain some degree of human liberty and can refuse to commit actions contrary to their conscience. But there are no limits for men who form part of a regularly organized government with an army under such discipline as prevails to-day. There are no crimes so revolting that men forming part of a government will not commit them at the wish of the man (Boulanger, Pugachëv, or Napoleon) who may chance to stand at its head.[15]

What Tolstoy has here in mind are crimes committed at home, in cities and villages, not in wars on the frontier or abroad. War is presented indeed, throughout *The Kingdom of God is within you* as only the ultimate expression, the finally degrading madness of the anonymous organised violence inherent in all state government. And it is notable that whereas the essay contains not a single live description of the degradation and injustices of war, it abounds in unforgettable descriptions of the debasing process of conscription (Tsarist-style) and of the use of conscripted troops to terrorise, to flog and if necessary to fire on, defenceless peasants who have dared to protest against the depredations of their landlords.

Tolstoy, as all his readers must know, cared nothing for politics as a profession or way of life or set of party attitudes to social problems. But as a result of a strange mixture of intellectual interests and psychological compulsions, he had been pressed into living and struggling with a political problem which most of us today would recognise as crucial to the survival of our civilisation. At what point, or under what specific forms, does the existence of centrally controlled armed forces – traditionally regarded as safeguards of every nation from attacks whether from without or within – tend instead both to corrupt the national life those forces are meant to guard, and also to provoke the attacks which they are intended to deter? Once he had recognised that this was *his* question, Tolstoy felt its implications too keenly, intimately and shamingly to weigh carefully the different answers that might be given to it. To recognise it was, for him, to answer it in the simplest, most sweeping, most Utopian terms. Whatever useful functions the state, as the controller of armed force and the guardian of public order, may once have played in creating sizeable economic and social units, once that task was done, it was inevitable that the state should deteriorate into an instrument of oppression at home and plunder abroad. Tolstoy presents this conclusion as a general political truth. But it is evident that, in reaching and expressing it, he had in mind his own nation, country and society. He believed that he had seen the political truth of nineteenth-century Russia; and often that truth seemed to him so deep-rooted as to be irremediable. All available blueprints for reform had been drawn up to meet the problems, or at least alleviate the evils, of countries and societies altogether unlike Russia – countries which Tolstoy disliked for that very reason, but also because their spokesmen presented them as models of what all other countries ought to be, but would also probably never quite succeed in becoming. Trapped in this impasse, Tolstoy vented the shame and rage which he felt for the political hopelessness of his own country in words which startle and stick because they were evidently chosen to hurt – to hurt his family, his friends, his peers, himself; to bruise or tarnish his own most idyllic memories of Russian life lest they should tempt him to close his eyes to the brutal political truth which underlay them. The result is a most formidable attack on internal or bureaucratic militarism. And perhaps the best way of suggesting its incisiveness is to compare it, on certain central issues, with the better-known accusations of Lenin. No two men could have attacked an existing social order for more different dogmatic premisses. It is surprising, therefore, how closely their accusations tally.

On the general nature of the state they are in almost complete agreement. Here, in one crisp sentence from *State Revolution* is Lenin's account. 'Under Capitalism we have a state in the proper sense of the word, that is, special machinery for the suppression of one class by another, and of the majority by the minority.' And here is Tolstoy's from *The Kingdom of God is within you*: 'Governments in our time – all of them, the most despotic and the liberal alike – have become organisations of violence employing four methods. The first and oldest is intimidation, the second is corruption, the third is. . .hypnotisation of the people, and the fourth [which Tolstoy proceeds to describe in his inimitable near-behaviourist fashion] is military enforcement.' Or, more succinctly: 'Armies are needed by governments to keep their subjects in submission and to exploit their labour.'[16] Again on the incompatibility of the state with generally accepted human ideals, and hence on the necessity of its 'withering away', they are equally at one, except that Tolstoy is more forthright and much more shocking. 'Christianity in its true sense', he writes at the opening of chapter 10 of *The Kingdom of God*, 'puts an end to the State. It was so understood from its very beginning, and for that Christ was crucified.'[17]And finally both these great Russians, for all their differences, were sensitive to the fact that their main enemy – the existing state of Russian society maintained by Tsarist violence – was, for all its terrible strength, strangely lifeless. Its grip on Russian men, women and children was, as if corpse-like, entirely incapable of loosening itself in response to persuasion, and yet surprisingly resistant to all normal forms and uses of force.

But with this last point of agreement, the comparability of the two great Russians ends abruptly and completely. To Lenin, the morbid stranglehold of Tsardom called for the most terrible of remedies. Let Tsardom plunge Russia into a general European war which would reveal its rottenness and weakness. Then a well-timed popular rising, with slogans to match the discontent of soldiers and civilians alike, together with the deft and ruthless use of a few dissident regiments, and the nightmare would soon be over. To Tolstoy, both the course of action which Lenin proposed and that which he was forced in fact to adopt would have seemed as terrible as the evil which he was claiming to replace and to cure. What exactly was Tolstoy's alternative?

It cannot be too often reiterated that Tolstoy was neither a prophet nor an advocate of organised non-violent resistance. Organised action, except of a philanthropic or educational kind, was not his forte. Moreover the forms of non-violent resistance which he did advocate, and the probable or possible effects which he attributed to them, are so little persuasive that one must wonder whether he himself really believed in them.[18] He offers a rather random list of things that a conscientious person should not do. Do not pay taxes which will be spent largely on the armed forces: resist – but non-violently – every act of governmental violence, every use of troops to back up police action; support every plea made by conscientious objectors to conscription. Act thus, and be prepared to suffer, as the early Christians did – and (and here Tolstoy's sermons have too often a pathetically wishful because earthly ending) perhaps your protest will inspire other protests, perhaps non-resistance will become widespread, perhaps because of this the whole filthy decrepit tsarist outfit will collapse like a pack of cards. Or perhaps (Tolstoy fails to add) Siberia will receive you. On the other hand it is important to notice that Tolstoy's individual pacifism is not motivated simply by the purist's wish to have no part in, and to be unsullied by, the workings of an evilly force-based régime. He seems to have believed that his own protests, combined with those of others whose beliefs he could not share or whose violent actions he deplored, *would* help to bring an end to Tsarist autocracy. He scornfully rejects the charges that he has disregarded the necessity of *some* method of maintaining public order, his point being that no method could be more intolerable than that which obtained in his own country. And he adds with commendable frankness that whether better forms of maintaining order, and achieving harmony and justice, can be easily devised is not immediately in question. The immediate imperative – and here Tolstoy is very close to the communists whom he so much disliked – is to help to get rid of the present system by any means that one's conscience allows one to employ.

But when all allowances are made, Tolstoy's diagnoses and accusations of political militarism remain distressingly weak on the practical side. If with Lenin every argument is geared to the possibilities and necessities of action, such considerations were with Tolstoy at best an after-thought, not something inherent to the truth he had to describe. In the light of its short term successes Lenin's 'activism' makes his particular diagnoses immensely persuasive: but in the longer term and in relation to his larger aims it has already given rise to doubts even among those from whom he compels admiration – who and what were his principal enemies? and how closely were his favoured methods related to the central vision and theory of Marxism? It seems to me possible that, contrariwise, the passage of time will reveal surprisingly lasting merits in Tolstoy's denunciations of political militarism.

In the first place, the fact that they are grounded in his curiously simplified theology, at least frees them from the characteristic biases and blindness of all the political ideologies of his age. Political – or domestic or bureaucratic – militarism is presented as always and everywhere, in whatever social and economic conditions, an appallingly insidious evil. It is evil not simply because it is liable to be unjustly and irresponsibly applied, but because, under the cloak of patriotism and defence, it tends to be applied arrogantly, hypocritically and brutally – and to brutalise both those who use it and those whom it cows and coerces. The means, the checks, the safeguards and the sacrifices needed to rescue a society that has fallen under militarist domination may well be more various, complex and indeed more violent than Tolstoy realised; but at least he deserves credit for having recognised the main moral symptoms of the disease. He does not simply pelt war and oppression with ugly epithets: he points to their roots in the very centre of social life as we know it. But secondly, as we should expect, he has left us in *The Kingdom of God is within you*, as in a number of his late essays and tales, some incomparably telling sketches – almost snapshots – of political militarism in practice, sketches that are the more telling because they contain elements – not simply the echoes – of that universal affection for humanity even at its worst, which is character-istic of the great Russian novelists. One such sketch, from the opening pages of the long 'Conclusion' of *The Kingdom of God is within you*, has a force such as no piece of directed propaganda could possibly have achieved. It communicates, incomparably, the pathos and the horror of an evil to which human society is always liable, an evil which we can all recognise, as if by the prompting of instinct, even if we have not been forced to witness it in the madness of war or behind the legal trappings of peace.

In the course of his relief work in the Tula and Ryazan provinces, Tolstoy ran into a train-load of soldiers, waiting at a wayside station, one fine September morning. They were on their way, under the com-mand of a provincial governor, and armed with rifles, ammunition and rods, to flog and kill some of the very peasants – suffering from a severe famine – whom Tolstoy was trying to assist. The particular peasants whom the soldiers were to deal with had protested against the seizure, by an avaricious young landlord, of a small wood which had traditionally been regarded as common land; and in the interests of law and order the soldiers were being brought in, with their rifles and rods, to restore public order, although corporal punishment had been declared illegal in Russia some thirty years earlier. Tolstoy describes the scene at the wayside station in his usual near-behaviourist style, and with the briefest and most restrained touches of comment. Most of the soldiers, young conscripts, 'in their clean new uniforms were standing about in groups, or sitting with their legs dangling from the wide-open doors of the trucks. Some were smoking, others nudging one another, joking. . .Others were cracking sunflower seeds, self-confidently spitting out the husks. . .laughing and chattering, as is natural to healthy, good-natured young fellows travelling. . .in lively company.' And thereupon Tolstoy adds: 'They went to the murder of their hungry fathers and grandfathers just as if they were going on some gay, or at any rate on quite ordinary, business.' And a similar impression was produced by the officers and police officials scattered about the platform and the first-class refreshment room. All seemed entirely pleased with themselves. All, 'on their way to murder or torture the hungry and defenceless creatures who provided them with their sustenance, had an air of being firmly convinced that they were doing their duty. They were even rather proud of themselves – "swaggering" about it.'[19]

With this scene as a fresh starting-point, Tolstoy reiterates the main arguments of his essay. But it is the scene itself, compounded of elements of innocence and good-nature, of self-satisfaction, and social conform-ism, and with the hideous reality in the background like an autumn storm, which convinces us. Something of the same sort, perhaps less blatantly, can and does occur in all political communities: we have been shown then *one* aspect, no doubt only one aspect, of the state at work. In this particular instance, Tolstoy tells us later, the horror was prevented. 'A lady of liberal tendencies' made a violent protest to the officer in charge; others (including, it would seem, Tolstoy) joined in. The officer was impressed; telephone messages were sent: the soldiers were given new orders – to cut down the wood and stack it pending a new judicial inquiry: the peasants were temporarily reprieved. But Tolstoy, rightly, tells us this part of the story hurriedly, almost apolo-getically. For it is not the (temporary and local) reprieve that mattered and that the reader remembers; but the possibilities of state terror in action or readiness for action, of state terror embodied in a few score of young men most of whom would be incapable of doing, for his own petty personal profit, a one-hundredth part of what the provincial governor was prepared to do, each of whom indeed would be insulted at the suggestion that he was capable of anything of the kind in his private life. And yet here they were, within a half-hour's journey from the place where they would have been forced to do it.[20]

It is as if, in this simple scene, a parable in itself, Tolstoy had not only claimed but proved to us: This is what war comes out of. Here is the preparation for war in what we call a country at peace. War is only the last climax of an infection that runs through every political society, liable to poison even the strongest and healthiest, the happiest and most kindly of its members. This is the truth which every human being must learn to see behind all political appearances and learn to say to himself in the face of all political clichés. Then and only then could there be that peace, 'the promised Kingdom of God, towards which the heart of every man aspires'.

# 6

## CONCLUDING REMARKS

Before the eighteenth century, such theorising as had been attempted in the field of international relations had been based on the simple picture of peace and war as a seemingly endless alternation or ding-dong between rival political powers. The only possible exceptions to this alternation were, it appeared, of two widely different kinds. There was the dream of a universal empire in which, following general conquest, permanent peace would be established throughout what men called 'the known world'; and there was the nightmare of a world entirely given over to war, to war between peoples and within peoples, of a 'time of troubles' so pervasive that no part or aspect of human life would be left unharmed by it. During the eighteenth, and for the most part during the nineteenth century, the dream of universal empire was quiescent; the plurality of comparably powerful European states – and later the rise of new great extra-European powers – weighed heavily against it. At the same time the nightmare picture of a universal time of troubles seemed equally unrealistic: only a few prescient thinkers (Engels and Tolstoy among them) being driven to reconsider it in the last decades of the nineteenth century. For these reasons, most nineteenth-century thinking about international relations – despite the practical wisdom often shown by governments and the idealistic aims of many individuals, societies and congresses dedicated to the cause of peace – remained rooted in the traditional conception, the seemingly endless alternation of peace and war, whether this was taken as the starting-point for explanatory theory or as the target for curative action.

Despite their great differences, the thinkers whom we have been considering were at one in reacting against the above traditional assumption. Or rather, each in his own way added to it a new depth, a new dimension, and certain new possibilities of interpretation and evaluation which have begun to transform it beyond recall, although the final picture, which will replace it, is still far from clear. War and peace can never again be thought about as occurrences comparable in their regularity to the changes of the seasons, or to the rhythm of bodily processes and feelings, which have so long provided the basic analogies for our conceptions of them. They have been made subject to wider comparisons, to searching analysis, mental manipulation and experiment – in a word to genuine thought guided by powerful human feeling. I want now to reconsider each of our writers, very briefly, from this point of view.

With Kant the new interpretation took the form of a hope, so hedged about by balancing qualifications, that its revolutionary import has only of late been clearly recognised. Formally – or in terms of his philosophical system – it rests on a notable extension, or at least reapplication, of his claim that Reason is as much the source of all practical, as of all theoretical, principles. Just as Reason requires that men shall form states and obey their laws – since only under the protection of effectively enforced laws can men live and develop together as free, rational and moral equals – so it demands that states shall desist from using their enforcement powers (their armies) to damage and destroy each other, under the pretence of obtaining justice from or punishing each other. That to take immediate steps toward this end is an imperative demand of Reason; that such steps can succeed only if certain delusive goals – world-government or peace-enforcement – are abjured; that the achievement of the ideal of world-peace depends upon the endless conquest and reconquest of human temptations and obstacles, and can never be completely secure – these, for Kant, are the essential facets of that conception of a 'legal relationship between states' which was to open up an entirely new chapter in the history of human aspiration and endeavour. Abstract as all this sounds, it amounts, at the theoretical level, to a notable change, or at least heralded change, in the ways men can, should and (as Kant believed) will come to think of peace and war, and of the international dimension of the never-ending human predicament and struggle.

In propounding and defending this belief Kant was as assured as the most 'statist' of his disciples, that the state is an indispensable prerequisite of any moral improvement of mankind, whether personal or professional, local, national or cosmopolitan. This assumption has often been regarded as characteristically German; but with Kant, as later with, for example, both Clausewitz and Hegel, it is to be attributed rather to that strand in Enlightenment thinking which maintained that all moral movement must spread from the top downward – from the state and the classes which most directly supported it to the broad popular masses. Tolstoy and the Marxists, from their very different first principles, repudiated this assumption entirely. For them the essential business of the state was oppression, for which war, or the so-called 'defence of the fatherland', provided the best possible excuse in the way of men and weapons. With the Marxists this doctrine was complicated in various ways by their class-analyses of all social tensions and conflicts. With Tolstoy, who was faced by a society stratified in an extremely simple way for expressly military purposes, this account of the state takes on a corresponding simplicity. So far from the state being a necessary precondition of all moral progress, as Kant and his followers supposed, it is, rather, the cause of the grossest evil, of the most corrupting falsity, the most loathsome hypocrisy among the rulers and degrading hypnotisation of the masses, in all modern nations. The state is a means of mass oppression: its main instrument is armed force; and the stock excuse for maintaining armed force – the existence of other highly armed rival states – terminates in the supreme evil: the mindless mass-murder that is war.

Clausewitz's aim was to supply an entirely objective analysis of war as a social phenomenon. Consequently the questions of its moral tolerability or practical replaceability – whether on general grounds supplied by Reason, as with Kant, or because of war's corrupting influence upon society, as with Tolstoy – are nowhere raised in *On War*. Nevertheless Clausewitz contributed through his objective analyses much that has a bearing on both Kant's and Tolstoy's philosophies of peace and war. In the first place he pointed to the immense variety of ways in which, and causes for which, wars have been fought, and urged that the key to the character of any particular war must be sought in the political situation, aims and decisions which give rise to it. Moreover he stressed that the more weighty, the more popularly backed the relevant political aims and decisions are, the more extreme – the more audacious, bloody, destructive and costly – the resulting war will tend to be. For this reason it is impossible to treat war as a relatively simple exercise, subject to certain fixed rules, laws, and used for relatively simple ends. It is inconceivable that war can ever be made into, or ever be based upon, a science. On the contrary it is an (apparently) permanent aspect of political and social life, closely connected with the competitive life of peoples, so that every particular war must be prepared for, planned, and executed as an element in a highly complex social context. No doubt both Kant and Tolstoy would have admitted that this was true:

but they did not recognise, or did not sufficiently emphasise, how much it must affect the seeming simplicity of their conclusions.

While Clausewitz pointed out in general, and mostly negative, terms that there could be no such thing as a sheer state of war between two adversaries, the Marxists discovered (or claimed to discover) an unexpectedly positive sting in the tail of this important truism. Applying their class-analysis of all political interests, movements and conflicts, Engels, and following him Lenin, argued in effect as follows. All wars are fought (see Clausewitz) to advance or defend the interests of the governments and governing classes of the states concerned. But in all serious wars the majority, on either side, feel themselves considerably involved; and in every really serious war the majority begins to see that its interest in the war divides it almost as much from its rulers as from the rulers of the alleged enemy. Whenever, therefore, the majority on either side becomes completely involved (as in Clausewitz's Absolute War) the war is ready to pass into revolution. This is, no doubt, to bowdlerise Clausewitz. But it has the theoretical merit of presenting war as a key term within a sociology of class interests and conflict: that is, within a system of ideas which could be utilised in advance to interpret possibilities, whispers or preparations of war or even to anticipate developments in a war already under way. Crude though the Marxist sociology of war may have been, it was the first sociology of war ever devised: and as such it contains the hope that, even if it has to be corrected and supplemented beyond recognition, it may some day help men to anticipate and forestall wars, instead of simply awaiting them with frictive anxiety or unleashing them on a gambler's impulse. In fine, the Marxist sociology of war was as impressive in its concern and intellectual ambition, as it was – and is – imperfect in its theoretical content.

Thus, whether in terms of the fundamental norms of human thought and action, or of the peculiar genius of the activity of war, or of war's corrupting influence upon civil society, or of its roots in and reaction against conflicts that arise from different forms of the division of labour, each of our authors deepened, widened, and rendered more articulate and more intellectually manageable traditional ways of thinking (or perhaps it would be better to say of non-thinking) about the seemingly endless alternation of peace and war throughout recorded history. That our authors should have done this in their very different ways is cause enough for studying them severally; but can they be said to have made any common contribution to this vital area of historical and social study? If they did, then it was certainly not an intended or conscious common contribution – if we except the Marxists' use (or abuse) of Clausewitz's central teaching. Nevertheless it seems to me that they probably contributed more, in their relative isolation from each other, to our understanding of peace and war than any school or succession of enquirers or publicists could possibly have done. Their widely differing and often sharply opposed standpoints could not conceivably have produced a single clear line of doctrine or of consistent action. But they were capable of producing, and may yet produce, a stimulating, fruitful and even saving debate on the different aims and claims which any international theory must seek, if not to reconcile, at least to set in intelligible and improvable relations one to another. Let us recall, again very briefly, how our authors help us to criticise and correct each other's characteristic teachings and assumptions.

If we want to criticise Kant's account of the conditions of a perpetual peace, then both Tolstoy and the Marxists are to hand to insist that his daring conception of a new international order – and behind this, of Reason's demand that the concept of legality be widened to apply intelligibly to the actions of states – rests upon the absurdly credulous assumption that every state is, at least potentially, a justice-producing institution and indeed a necessary instrument of progress in Enlightenment and culture. Kant of course counters this accusation, admitting that in truth all states commit terrible injustices but maintaining that they can only conceivably become less evil as the main excuse for their arbitrary abuses of force – the constant danger of war – is progressively weakened: a development which, in turn, is conceivable only as the advantages of a new international order gradually come to be recognised by even the most backward and arbitrarily governed of states. If, on the other side, we wish to criticise the Marxists, Kant is to hand with the powerful claim that they have simply failed to recognise the distinctive and permanent character of the international problems – namely that conflict of interest will always arise between communities that acknowledge no common political authority. And if we wish to criticise Tolstoy's claim that the state and its fullest manifestation in war are built on lies – the state in truth being an instrument of sheer oppression, and war an imbecilic confusion into which governments drive their subjects – Kant and Clausewitz will remind us that, although all states may be evil and war is always a bloody and brutal business, both have other aspects as well: the state being necessary for the enforcement of justice, and wars beginning, not with the ruthless aggressor (who would always prefer to grab and destroy, unopposed) but with the 'weak defender' who decides to make a stand for survival. Finally, if we wish to criticise Clausewitz, all our authors are to hand to accuse him of accepting as a permanent element in human life an institution whose dependence upon other forces he was the first to recognise clearly. But, in turn, our other authors must accept from Clausewitz the almost equally pertinent rejoinder: that in almost all human endeavours some degree of enforcement, some degree of risk-taking, some inevitable mistakes and mistimings due to imperfect information will always persist, and that on this score the study of war offers us lessons, no matter how brutally embodied, which are relevant to the whole realm of social action.

All these lines of argument and counter-argument would admit of endless elaboration and specification: each helps us to engage with difficulties which too much international theory is content to avoid: each retains a pertinence to the international problems which face mankind today. It is important that we should recognise clearly the nature of that continuing pertinence. It is political, not technological or economic. The thinkers whom we have been studying lived and developed their thoughts towards the end of a period, roughly equatable with the Age of Enlightenment, during which most European governments greatly increased their power, and their citizens notably extended their political, economic and cultural aspirations, but specifically military skills and methods remained relatively unchanged. Only in the later writings of Engels, and perhaps of Tolstoy, did we find a recognition of the fact that this period had ended, and that a new period, in which issues of peace and war would be dominated by economic needs and technological improvisation, had begun. In our century this development has of course been carried forward, farther and faster than any nineteenth-century mind could have believed possible; so that today almost all thinking about our topic proceeds in terms of competing military technologies, and behind them, of rival economic systems.

But the ideas and decisions upon which the future, and indeed the survival, of mankind will depend, will be political, not technological. The prodigious technological advances of our age, most obviously in the nuclear field, but also potentially in the fields of economic, biological and chemical warfare, have affected the central political issue of peace and war in only one fundamental way. They have falsified Clausewitz's claim that, as between comparable adversaries, the most logical way of fighting, for either side, is to escalate or maximise one's efforts with a view to achieving absolute victory, or at least to threatening one's adversary with absolute defeat. Nuclear warfare, and modern delivery systems, have put a ceiling upon the efficacy of any such escalations of destructive effort. Beyond a certain point (assuming adversaries of at all comparable capability) they become counter-productive because certainly suicidal. But apart from this one immensely significant, though as yet almost wholly unexploited change, military developments have been very much as Kant, and later Engels and others, foresaw that they would be: wars have become vastly more expensive, vastly more destructive, vastly more demoralising for those responsible for them or directly engaged in them, vastly more menacing to the future of mankind. In this situation the questions posed – if not the positions defended – by our authors remain as politically stimulating as ever, each suggesting powerful criticisms of easy answers to the others, even if none of them has itself received a wholly persuasive answer. Can and should international theory be focussed upon the abjuration of the right to go to war by all (in the first instance by certain like-minded) states? Or should it rather be aimed at the elimination of certain evidently intolerable ends, styles, and methods of warfare? (Was Kant right, not only against Vattel, but against most liberal and most Marxist publicists of our century?) On what principles, if any, can wars be graded, as more or less tolerable, and less or more destructive? Can a government ever be certain that a war, no matter how sanely limited in the initial intention, will in fact be contained within those limits? Are wars, even if sometimes occasioned by other causes, of particular significance in our epoch in relation to rival – whether rising or falling, progressive or restrictive – forms of economic production and distribution? And do militaristic standards and methods, whenever they are introduced into civilian life, inevitably corrupt it? These are certainly questions which any serious student of international relations must have at the forefront of his mind. But where do they take him? Do they offer him even partial guidance? If our authors, considered together, came near to setting up a genuine intellectual debate in place of a shapeless battle of opinions, is this the most that we can hope to gain from them? Or – to indulge in a moment's whimsicality – can we take our leave of them by imagining them, in some variant of the Elysian fields, tirelessly disputing, endlessly criticising and correcting one another, each no doubt using his adversaries' arguments and criticisms as whetstones for his own, each in this way stimulating the others to better, more persuasive statements of their respective cases, but with no hope or prospect of ever achieving, or even approaching, ultimate agreement?

There was a time when I believed that in serious political controversy one could look for no other outcome or success than this. But I will confess that I now find this position, although salutary against most forms of political evangelism, too intellectually self-denying to be practically acceptable. Endless, even if endlessly clarifying, debate over the concepts of war and peace carries too much of the aroma of fiddling while Rome burns. Nor is the position just described a fitting response to, a warm enough reception and assimilation of, the heroic intellectual efforts of our chosen authors.

A better response is to ask, in the broadest terms, where they failed or at least fell short, and where, by giving a new twist to the debate which they initiated, we could point it in a more promising direction. I will therefore conclude by outlining two areas of enquiry, which all my authors seem in certain passages to be on the verge of recognising and opening up, but then fall away from, as if they were too strange, too intellectually unexplored and unpopulated, too much a philosophical wilderness or wonderland.

The first can be suggested in very simple terms. All political philosophy since Plato, has been directed to articulating the criteria of good – or at least of tolerable – political life *within* a given state or city. (Plato in one passage goes so far as to urge that the ideal state will either have no neighbours or at least no contacts with its neighbours, so as to be free of all contingent influences and intrusions.) The good state, therefore, has meant the state that is good *viz-à-viz* its subjects or citizens, for all that, in fact, every state that ever existed has had to face not only its own citizens but other neighbouring and probably rival states, and indirectly the citizens of those states as well. The result is that no political philosopher has ever dreamed of looking for the criteria of a good state *viz-à-viz* other states – in the way in which a good family man can also be a good neighbour. It might be retorted, of course, that the task here suggested is an impossible one in view of the variety, multiplicity and contingency of a state's external relations. But I suspect that this retort betrays weaknesses to which even the most strenuous philosophers are liable: a dislike of venturing into territories in which they find the tracks of no forerunner, and a disinclination to move from intellectual positions which have become so habitual that the effort to change them could be both painful and undignified. Kant came closer than any other philosopher to putting the simple question: what would it be for a state to be 'good at' external relations? But his answer, although so original, was also, as we have seen, disappointingly negative and palpably incomplete. To fill out, and at the same time to generalise, Kant's answer seems to me a prime task of political philosophy today. And it would also help us to see more clearly what is lacking in both Marxist and Anarchist criticisms of the state.

The second area of enquiry which, as it seems to me, our authors bring us in sight of, is less simple, but can be described more briefly. It is astonishing that none of our authors (and again that Kant in particular) should not have felt the need of an overall survey of the different possible – differently defensible or indefensible – uses of force in human life. If each could have presented his views within the framework which such a survey could provide, how much more easily those views could have been argued and tested and criticised and improved. In particular, for the purpose of our topic, such a survey should concentrate on those crucial conceptual divides – points, lines or hazy no-man's-lands – where competition (which is surely endemic in all life) passes into conflict and coercion, and where coercion passes into intolerable oppression and war. It seems to me more than strange, it seems to me ominous, that so little philosophical work has been done on these vital questions, which are central to the international theorising not only of Kant, but of Clausewitz, the Marxists and Tolstoy.

So my final commendation of these great men is to suggest questions which they did not raise, and thought-adventures on which they did not embark. But there is no dispraise in this. However it may be in other spheres of life – the artistic, the religious, or the pursuit of purely theoretical truth – in political thought and endeavour a man's rewards are with the living, and his work is approved not by any finality of achievement, but in terms of further tasks and problems, further efforts and anxieties, dangers and rescues, which it makes possible. Thus, if our authors are to achieve the success which their thoughts on peace and war deserve, it lies with us to pursue their thoughts further and to add more grist to their mills.

# BIBLIOGRAPHICAL NOTE

None of Kant's bibliographers, biographers or critical expositors have shown an adequate interest in, or appreciation of, his political writings. Even such intelligent and imaginative expositors of Kant as Ernst Cassirer and A. D. Lindsay have brushed *Perpetual Peace* aside as an amateurish sketch, of interest only (in Cassirer's judgement) for its exemplification of the central tenets of the Critical Philosophy. Of more recent expositions of Kant by political theorists and historians, a number are mentioned in my text (above) and in the references (below); and of these the following, despite their differences in detailed interpretation, can be recommended to serious students of Kant's political philosophy: F. H. Hinsley, chapter 4 of *Power and the Pursuit of Peace* (CUP 1963) and chapter 5 of *Nationalism and the International System* (Hodder & Stoughton 1973); Peter Gay, *The Enlightenment* vol. II *passim* (Weidenfeld & Nicolson 1966); and S. J. Hemleben, *Plans for World Peace through Six Centuries*, pp. 87ff (Chicago University Press 1943). An article by the distinguished political philosopher K. N. Waltz, 'Kant, Liberalism and War' in the *American Political Science Review* (LVI, 2 (1962) 331–40) is perceptive and thought-provoking but mistaken in one central issue; while a small volume of essays, *La Philosophie Politique de Kant* (Presses Universitaires de France 1962) interestingly links the teachings of *Perpetual Peace* with Kant's philosophy of law and philosophy of history.

Kant's various political writings have appeared in English, sporadically and in the main with utterly inadequate introductions, in a number of editions since his death. Quite the best and most easily available collection is *Kant's Political Writings*, edited by H. Reiss, translated by H. Nisbet (CUP 1970). All my references to *Perpetual Peace* and related writings are to this edition.

The bibliography of Clausewitz in German is very extensive, but its most important items are covered in the critical apparatus ('Manuscripts, Books and Articles cited') of Professor Peter Paret's *Clausewitz and the State*, pp. 445ff (OUP 1976), and in the bibliography, provided at the end of vol. II, of Professor Raymond Aron's *Penser la guerre, Clausewitz* (Gallimard, Paris 1976. I have referred to both these works in a number of places in my text. They are contributions to Clausewitzian scholarship comparable to those of the great Hans Delbrück, of Hans Rothfels and

Professor W. Hahlweg in German. Professor Aron's book provides a comprehensive, sympathetic and uniformly wise survey of all the theoretical problems that arise from studying *On War*; Professor Paret's provides the indispensable social background for a just appreciation of it.

There are two currently available English translations of *On War*: Colonel J. J. Graham's three volume version (Routledge & Kegan Paul) first published early in this century, has been reprinted no fewer than nine times, which testifies to its readability. Unfortunately it conveys no impression of the smooth style of the original and in places it could easily mislead the modern reader. The recent translation, in one volume, by Professor Michael Howard and Professor Peter Paret (Princeton University Press 1976) reads much more smoothly and, although I would question it in places, is much more reliable. I have decided to give references to both these translations throughout.

It goes almost without saying that there is no one agreed and comprehensive coverage of sources, and no generally esteemed critical survey, of classic Marxist thought on the central topic of this book. A good first study, in English, was provided by S. Neumann's 'Engels and Marx: Military Concepts of the Social Revolutionaries', in *Makers of Modern Strategy*, edited by Edward Mead Earle (Princeton University Press 1943); and there is a growing literature, connected with our topic, in German. What is lacking, however, and what will not easily be forthcoming, given prevailing ideological divisions, is a general acceptance of the following essential distinction in research interests. First there is the philosophical question of the adequacy of Marxist general theory as a basis for a theoretical study of peace and war between peoples. The materials for this task present no problem: they are to be found in the acknowledged master-texts of Marxist theory. But secondly, there is the much more specific, indeed the historical question of the effectiveness of the response of Marxist theorists to particular problems, opportunities and dangers, for instance those that faced Engels in the late 1880s and early 1890s.

For the latter the basic materials can be found in Gustav Mayer's *Friedrich Engels, Eine Biographie* (Martinus Nighoff, The Hague 1934). This work was translated and abridged a few years later as *Friedrich Engels, a Biography*, translated by G. and H. Highett and edited by R. H. S. Crossman. This translation is particularly full and useful for Engels' concern with a general European war during his last years; but unfortunately it contains no account of the available sources, and for this reason I have referred, in my text, to the German edition. More recently, a number of these sources have been made more fully available by the publication (as yet unfortunately only in German) of Engels' main writings on military topics: *Friedrich Engels Ausgewählte Militarische Schriften* (Deutscher Militarverlag, Berlin 1964). This important work, in two volumes, contains the complete text of the article of 1893 'Kann Europa abrusten?', and a number of items indicating the beginnings and development of Engels' politico-military interests. It is to be hoped that it will soon be made available in English.

# NOTES

### Chapter 1 Introductory (pp. 1–7)

1 *Kant's Political Writings* ed. H. Reiss (CUP 1970) p. 47.
2 *Diplomatic Investigations* ed. H. Butterfield & M. Wight (Allen & Unwin 1966) p. 20.
3 For a clear account of this literary scandal see R. Aron *Penser la guerre, Clausewitz* (Gallimard, Paris 1976) vol. 1 p. 176.

### Chapter 2 Kant on Perpetual Peace (pp. 8–36)

1 The title of Kant's pamphlet 'Zum ewigen Frieden' is doubly ambiguous. It succeeds in suggesting three possible meanings which no single English phrase can convey; roughly 'concerning Perpetual Peace', 'towards Perpetual Peace' and '*at* Perpetual Peace' i.e. the peace of the graveyard, as Kant ruefully points out.
2 This view is assumed by those of Kant's critics who repeatedly complain that his proposals provide no immediate safeguard against the existence or threat of aggression. These critics should *read* his pamphlet.
3 Professor K. N. Waltz, in his otherwise perceptive 'Kant, Liberalism and War' (*American Political Science Review* LVI, 2 (1962) 331–40) falls into this error, as does M. Campbell Smith in his introduction to *Kant's Perpetual Peace* (1903), cited in Hinsley, *Power and the Pursuit of Peace* (CUP 1963) p. 374.
4 This is assumed by all those who see in *Perpetual Peace* an anticipation of the League of Nations idea, e.g. by C. J. Friedrich in his introduction to *Inevitable Peace* (1945) (and in many later essays) and by E. J. Hobsbawm, *The Age of Reason* (Weidenfeld & Nicolson 1962).
5 Witness the inclusion of *Perpetual Peace* in a notable recent collection of pacifist literature, *The Pacifist Conscience*, ed. P. Mayer (Penguin 1966).
6 Reiss p. 95.
7 Even Professor Hedley Bull seems to fall into this error. See *Diplomatic Investigations* ed. Butterfield and Wight p. 48. So does C. J. Friedrich in his 'L'Essai sur la Paix' in *La Philosophie Politique de Kant* (Presses Universitaires de France 1962).

8 Reiss pp. 93ff.
9 Ibid. pp. 98ff.
10 See F. H. Hinsley (1963) ch. 4.
11 For an excellent account of the development and collapse of Rousseau's international thinking, see Hinsley (1963) ch. 3 and notes.
12 Vattel's *Le Droit des Gens, ou Principes de la Loi Naturelle* has been reprinted in two volumes in the Carnegie Classics of International Law series. The crucial passages for the present discussion are to be found in vol. II livre III chs 2, 4 and 12.
13 Reiss p. 183.
14 Ibid. p. 170 §59.
15 This is Kant's general doctrine of the 'moral title'. See also his 'Theory and Practice' in Reiss pp. 61ff.
16 Reiss p. 98.
17 Ibid. p. 105.
18 Ibid. p. 170.
19 Ibid. pp. 129, 165, 171.
20 Ibid. p. 103.
21 Ibid. pp. 104 and 171.
22 Ibid. pp. 105ff.
23 Ibid. pp. 44–6 and 113–14.
24 Ibid. p. 112.
25 Ibid. p. 46.
26 Ibid. p. 112
27 Ibid. pp. 123–4.
28 Ibid. pp. 177–8.

*Chapter 3* Clausewitz on the Nature of War (pp. 37–65)

(References to Colonel J. J. Graham's translation of *On War* (Routledge & Kegan Paul) are signified as GT: references to the new translation by Professor Michael Howard and Professor Peter Paret (Princeton University Press 1976) are signified as HPT.

1 GT vol. I pp. xix and xx; HPT p. 63.
2 GT vol. I p. 121; HPT p. 149.
3 GT vol. I pp. 107ff; HPT p. 141.
4 GT vol. I pp. 121ff; HPT pp. 149ff.
5 GT vol. I pp. 117ff; HPT p. 147.
6 GT vol. I pp. 107–8; HPT p. 141.
7 GT vol. I p. 152; HPT p. 168.
8 GT vol. I p. 108; HPT p. 141.
9 GT vol. I p. 133; HPT p. 158.
10 GT vol. III pp. 77ff; HPT p. 577.
11 Ibid.
12 GT vol. I pp. 130ff; HPT pp. 156ff.
13 Cited by Dirk Blasius in *Carl von Clausewitz und de Hauptdenker des*

*Marxismus* (Wehrwissenschaftliche Rundschau 1966 Heft 5 & 6) p. 28. The original source is K. Marx and F. Engels *Werke* (Dietz Verlag) Bd 29 S.256.

14 This debate is admirably assessed in R. Aron, *Penser la guerre, Clausewitz* vol. 1 pts. 1 & 2, and in numerous appended notes.

15 GT vol. III pp. 79ff; HPT p. 579.

16 GT vol. I pp. 21ff; HPT pp. 86ff.

17 GT vol. III pp. 122ff; HPT pp. 605ff. I should point out that both Professor Aron and Professor Paret (in his *Clausewitz and the State*, OUP 1976) give a rather less radical assessment of the different stages of Clausewitz's thought than I do here. See especially Aron, pp. 88ff.

18 Professor Aron takes a very different view of this question. See vol. 1 pp. 360ff and 437ff.

19 This is the explanation of Clausewitz's otherwise almost unintelligible argument in Book 1 chapter 1 section 1. GT vol. I p. 1; HPT p. 75.

20 GT vol. II p. 409; HPT p. 516.

21 GT vol. I pp. 6ff; HPT pp. 78ff.

22 GT vol. I p. 33; HPT p. 93.

23 GT vol. I p. 45; HPT p. 99.

24 Professor Aron discusses this point illuminatingly: (1976) pp. 122–39.

25 GT vol. III p. 90; HPT p. 586.

26 See *Diplomatic Investigations*, ed. Butterfield & Wight, p. 194.

27 GT vol. II pp. 160–1; HPT p. 374.

28 Letter to Marie von Brühle, quoted by Paret (1976) p. 3.

29 GT vol. III p. 103; HPT p. 593.


*Chapter 4* Marx and Engels on Revolution and War (pp. 66–99)

1 Blasius (1966).

2 *Anti-Dühring* pp. 202ff in the Delisle Burns translation (Lawrence and Wishart 1936).

3 *The Origin of the Family, Private Property and the State* pp. 313ff in the Marx–Engels *Selected Works* vol. II (Foreign Language Publishing House Moscow; published in the UK by Lawrence and Wishart 1962).

4 *Grundrisse* (Pelican 1973) pp. 471–95.

5 Ibid. p. 476.

6 Ibid. p. 474.

7 Ibid.

8 *Anti-Dühring* pp. 117–18 and *The Role of Force in History* (*Marx–Engels Selected Works* vol. 3 p. 411).

9 *The Communist Manifesto* in Marx, *The Revolution of 1848* (Pelican 1974) p. 78.

10 Ibid. p. 76.

11 'Force and Economics in the Foundations of the German Empire', cited in *Marx–Engels Selected Correspondence* (Martin Lawrence, London 1934) p. 309. (Hereafter cited as *MESC.*)

12 *MESC* p. 309.

13 Blasius (1966) pp. 289–91.

14 Quoted in S. Naumann's 'Engels and Marx: Military Concepts of the Social Revolution', ch. 7 of *Makers of Modern Strategy* edited by Edward Mead Earle (Princeton University Press 1943).

15 *MESC* p. 434.

16 Ibid.

17 The argument from here to p. 88 was prompted by, but not derived from, Gustav Mayer's *Friedrich Engels, eine Biographie* (Martinus Nighoff, The Hague 1934), from whose English translation I have taken a number of quotations. I have, however, given references to the much fuller, and fully documented, German original for reasons explained in my Bibliographical Note at p. 143 above.

18 Mayer (1934) p. 469.

19 Ibid. p. 463.

20 *MESC* p. 455.

21 Ibid. pp. 456–7.

22 Mayer (1934) p. 515.

23 Ibid. p. 518.

24 Ibid. p. 514.

25 For Lenin's uses of Clausewitz to lambaste his fellow Marxists, see Blasius (1966) pp. 327ff.

### *Chapter 5* Tolstoy (pp. 100–32)

1 *War and Peace* (Penguin Classics) pp. 221ff.

2 See Paul Boyer, *Chez Tolstoy, entretiens à Iasnaïa Poliana* (Institut d'Etudes Slaves, Paris 1950) p. 40.

3 *War and Peace* (Penguin Classics) pp. 974ff.

4 Ibid. pp. 719, 810, 976, 1433ff.

5 Ibid. p. 207.

6 Ibid. pp. 716ff.

7 Ibid. pp. 978ff.

8 Ibid. p. 1420.

9 Ibid.

10 Ibid. p. 1423.

11 Ibid. pp. 920ff.

12 *The Kingdom of God and Peace Essays* (The World's Classics) pp. 468ff.

13 Ibid. pp. 488–9.

14 Ibid. pp. 443–4.

15 Ibid. p. 374.

16 Ibid. pp. 229–34.

17 Ibid. p. 281.

18 Ibid. pp. 264ff.

19 Ibid. pp. 347–8.

20 Ibid. p. 350.